THIS IS RACING

THIS IS

RICHARD CREAGH-OSBORNE
RACING
Tactics and Strategy in Action

Nautical

First published © 1977
by
United Nautical Publishers SA, Basle

This edition published © 1977
by
NAUTICAL PUBLISHING COMPANY Ltd
Nautical House, Lymington, Hampshire, England

in association with
George G Harrap & Co Ltd,
London

ISBN 0–245.53070.3

Reprinted - 1978

Colour separations and text setting by
Westerham Press, Westerham, Kent, England
Printing by Grafiche Pagano - Campomorone-Ge - Italy

Acknowledgements

A team of people have helped with the creation of this book. My thanks are due for their patience, diligence and expertise in their respective departments:

Peter A.G. Milne—most of the colour drawings
Keith Blount LSIA—graphic design and layouts
Elizabeth Smith—drawings
Joan Hancock—typing and correcting
Augusta Creagh-Osborne—correcting and picture filing
The staff of Nautical Publishing Company

I am also indebted to the following for the use of their photographs:

Bill Banks 0.1, 2.5, 2.8, 6.21, 9.7, 9.12, 10.1, 11.2, 11.5, 11.15, 11.28

La Noüe/Bateaux 0.2, 0.22, 2.1, 5.36, 11.10, 11.33, 12.4
Kurt Schubert 0.3, 0.14, 0.16, 3.1, 4.1
Ragnvalds Foto 0.9
Bob Fisher 0.10, 0.11, 0.15, 0.20, 0.23, 6.14, 6.35, 7.12, 9.2, 9.23, 10.6, 11.26, 13.1, 14.2, and title page
John Watney 0.19
Thierry Vigoureux/Bateaux 8.2
Isabelle Troublé/Bateaux 9.30, 13.5
D. Maupas/Bateaux 12.12

The Model photos were taken by the author and Keith Blount. All other photos are the author's, except 1.1, 8.1, 11.8 (anon).

My thanks are also due to large numbers of other people who have assisted in many small but vital ways.

Richard Creagh-Osborne
Lymington, 1976

Yacht racing is a huge subject which can comprise, not only the sailing of a boat in a race, but all the things which lead up to this. These include choosing a class to race in, designing, building and fitting out the boat, finding and training a crew, becoming expert in such things as boat and sail handling techniques, racing rules, strategy, tactics, weather lore, and even psychological preparation and physical fitness.

If this book was to cover all of this it would be so superficial in each part as to be of little practical value. It is a desire to give practical and useful advice, based on my own experience, that governs the limits that have been set.

I have assumed that the reader is sailing in a competitive boat, which means that it is capable of winning races. I also assume that the crew is able to handle the boat well and that it will be set-up and tuned adequately for the prevailing conditions. Given this—How does one actually win a race?

What does the successful crew need to know? What makes a crew *consistently* a winner in all types of conditions? How, first of all, does one start, get around the course and finish without hitting anyone?

This book gives some of the answers to these questions and, though beginners to racing are very much in mind, I am sure that even quite expert crews will find things here that they had not thought of before. Also, with the use of full colour, I have been able to show ideas in a more visually attractive and useful way.

The book is intended just as much for the proud owner of an *Optimist* pram dinghy as it is for the twelve-man crew of a *Class One* ocean racer and for anything in between. The point is that the most important part of our sport is common to all types of boats. Every yacht uses only the wind for propulsion, water to float on and the crew's own muscles to control the hull and rig. The rules are the same for all sizes of boat everywhere and so also are the basic principles of the tactics which stem from these rules.

To explain the way a race is run, how to plan your strategy for that race, how to learn the basic rules of the game and how to make the most of this knowledge to develop successful inter-boat tactics, how to enjoy sparring with competitors of like standards, these are the aims of this book.

Ninety-five per cent of sailors almost never win a race at any level and I suspect that at least a similar proportion have only a very hazy idea of the rules and of how the all-important wind is generated. It is for them this book is written as well as for the great number of other people who want to start racing but do not know how to do it and who are afraid of making fools of themselves on a race course.

Racing a boat should be fun! Learning exactly how to do it is the best way to take advantage of all the fun that is available.

How to use this book

The book is divided into three parts: First— the introduction which is intended for beginners to racing to help them to feel something of the atmosphere of a race. The illustrations are mainly colour photographs which are here only to amplify the text and to provide a window for looking into the heart of our sport.

Part Two contains a collection of basic and background information on a number of subjects. The rules of racing are discussed here in principle only—they are dealt with in more detail in Part Three though in this book the rules are not analysed. The main purpose is to show how the rules influence boat-to-boat tactics. There are many other things which also influence tactics including how the wind and currents work, the psychology of the crew and even the geometrical details of the course. Part Two covers these and much else which experience has shown can aid in the winning of races.

Part Three uses as a basis a fictitious race round a triangular course and takes the reader from before the start to after the finish. The purpose is to explain successful inter-boat tactics and to bring in the more important racing rules which are those which apply for more than ninety-five per cent of every race.

The racing rules are described only in a general way as they occur during the race and are cross-linked to the Appendix where their proper titles and numbers are listed. Also listed are books for further reading including some which analyse the racing rules in great detail and which can be used for solving tricky problems of right and wrong.

In this book my aim is to encourage crews to *think* and to give them enough knowledge to get them out onto the race course with a chance of winning—a very good chance indeed if they can absorb some of the advice it contains.

Contents

Contents (continued)

Part One

An Introduction to Racing

Setting the scene

A race is something you try to do fast. Some races are against the clock. A yacht race is against other yachts, usually at least nominally identical, crewed by anything from one person to up to ten or more, in size from a six foot long child's pram dinghy made by father in a few weekends up to a 100 foot long ocean-racer costing as much as many of us can earn in our whole working lives.

Yachts use only the wind for motive power. The wind is variable and, some say, is too chancy a power source for their liking preferring something akin to a huge power fan at one end of a lake. But for the true sailor it is the variety of wind and water conditions and the mutual pitting of wits, expertise, knowledge and intuition which makes it such a fascinating sport.

There is no doubt that yachts can be expensive to keep, and racing yachts are the most expensive of all. It has been said that the yacht is 'a hole in the water into which you pour money' and that ocean-racing is like 'standing under a cold shower for forty-eight hours tearing up 100 dollar bills'. There is more than a grain of truth in this but it is more nearly true that it doesn't matter what size the boats are as long as they are all the same. Some of the finest and most exciting racing takes place in *Optimist* dinghies, *Sunfish* surfboards or *Laser* single-handers.

The ballyhoo associated with *Class One* ocean-racers may be essential to the owner and his team of experts because, after all, he has paid a huge sum for his sport and he needs a return in publicity if nothing else. Similarly the more recent tendency, regrettable to many, for some keen classes to be dominated by near-professionals or works-backed boats needs well publicized success to feed it. There is no doubt that it is modern communications, publicity and advertising which has changed, and will continue to change this 'sport for the leisured amateur' into the world-wide, money-orientated, ever more professional game that it is today, at least in the keener classes where most is at stake.

Fortunately the sport has many levels and good fun can be had at all of them. The first thing to decide is WHO and WHAT are YOU? Where do you, yourself, fit into all this?

It is possible to fit into almost any level of this sport whether you are wealthy or not. If you have no money to spare you can still take part at the very expensive end—but you have to be good!

But how does one start if one knows nothing except how to sail a boat? One way is to buy your way in. It all depends on how much you want to spend. A fully equipped international two-man racing centreboarder (*0.1*) might cost you as much as a small european-type car and then you would have

0.1   470 class international two-man centreboarders

0.2　Offshore racers in a hard wind

to pay for the expenses of a crew and the cost of travel, measuring certificates, club subscriptions and fees etc in order to campaign it. If you were racing most weekends you could easily spend half as much again in a year. If you went abroad with the boat then it could be much more.

You might buy an offshore-racer (*0.2*) and employ an expert to find and organise a crew. These boats come in sizes ranging commonly from over 70 feet overall down to 22 feet or so with crews from say, fifteen down to three. You could pay almost anything to run a *Class One* boat for a year but a boat in one of the smaller classes could be less than the cost of the International dinghy to campaign as long as you did not take it abroad. The first cost of a small *Quarter-tonner* might be from three to six times the cost of the Inter-

national dinghy, fully equipped.

But do not despair. You could build an 11 foot *Mirror* or an *Optimist* dinghy (*0.3*) in a few weekends for about £150 ($400), join a small local club for as little as £5 and race it in the club fleet for practically nothing. You would probably have just as much fun, possibly more, but you would be unlikely to get your name in the papers or, if successful, be wooed by this or that sail-loft or clothing manufacturer to use their products (for free, of course).

In between there are a host of levels at which you can aim. There are purely local club classes of all sizes which tend to be the cheapest of their type both to buy and to race. Then there are 'National' classes with a national organisation which has to be paid for. These often run Area or National Championships at different places where you can meet and race against crews of an inevitably higher standard of experience and expertise. Also the standard of tuning and fitting out of the boats will tend to be higher and hence more expensive.

But it is when one aspires to the 'International' or internationally distributed classes that the cost in time as well as money begins to sky-rocket. The former is the term for classes which are specially recognised and controlled by the International Yacht Racing Union, the controlling body of the international sport. They inevitably attract publicity, especially those used in the Olympic Games every four years. This in turn attracts some, although not all, of the most talented crews and draws in the 'go-fast' manufacturers.

Yacht racing is still a considerable art though boat-speed and slick handling can be predicted or ensured by clever sail making and ever more refined gear such as winches, spars, rigging controls

0.3 Small children learn to race in Optimist dinghies

and, in the ocean-racing classes, instruments. There is a constant battle among the inventive semi-commercial core of semi-professional crews to devise better boats and equipment.

Many successful sailors, often arising out of the tough school of dinghy racing, join commercial firms and, apart from their general advice and special expertise, a part of their job is to be associated with winning. In this way the firm's sails, winches, clothing or whatever get promotion. Some sailmaking firms in particular are run by groups of racing sailors who often specialise in sails for only one, or a small number of classes, and they then campaign in these classes themselves

as amateurs.

The standards of expertise and efficiency are rising all the time under the pressures, not only of healthy competition between friendly sportsmen, but as a result of commercial backing and often aided and abetted by owners and crews who see a way to outstrip their rivals in the next big race by the purchase of some new sail or piece of go-fast gear, or even a complete new boat or the services of an expert at tuning or tactics.

These are the indisputable facts of the way the top level of yacht racing is moving but the message is 'If you can't stand the heat—get out of the kitchen!'

0.4   An offshore racer needs a big crew who work together as a team

Fortunately there are indeed many levels and many grades of heat in our sport and each must decide where he fits into this world-embracing pattern.

You might become one of those valuable people who specialise in one aspect of the sport and then your sailing need cost you next to nothing. Go to your nearest or chosen club and ask the secretary to put you on the 'crews list'. A steady crewing job in a dinghy can lead eventually to a good crew being able to get almost any sort of berth he could want in any part of the world, sometimes with all expenses paid (*0.4*). An expert skipper has even been known to advertise for a crew, with the prize of a near certain Olympic gold medal for the successful and dedicated applicant.

So it is up to you! We are talking here about racing. Not cruising or pottering or motor-boating or one of the many other aspects of the use of boats but—racing. You have to set your sights on your target, at whatever level you decide, and then go for it!

What is a Race?

There are two totally different aspects to a sailing race and, at their highest pitch of perfection, they are combined in a truly fascinating way to form the basis of a complicated but utterly rewarding sport.

Reduced to its simplest it can be stated that a race is won by the boat which goes from the start to the finish in the shortest time (*0.5*). In the absence of all other boats, and without interference of any sort, the problem for the skipper and crew is how to keep the boat moving at its fastest speed on the various points of sailing encountered on each 'leg' of the course and also to work out exactly which is the fastest course to the finish.

The way to achieve top boat-speed is a subject dealt with in another book*; here we are concerned with the nature of a race in theory and practice including the rules of the race and how to use them to win.

A point to note at an early stage is that the geometrically shortest course is not necessarily the fastest. There are many influences which affect this such as relative wind strength in different areas of the course, wind shifts which can be predicted, variations in currents and also sea and wave conditions.

The type of boat being sailed must also be considered. For example, how fast is it? Can point 'A' be reached before the tide turns? Is it large enough to take in its stride the waves in area 'B' (*0.6*) or must they be avoided by means

Boat Tuning for Speed – Imhoff & Pranger.

0.5 ▲ *A start for cruiser/racers*

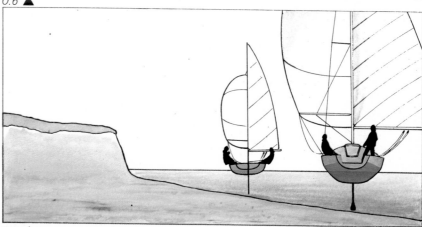

0.6 ▲

0.7 ▲

5

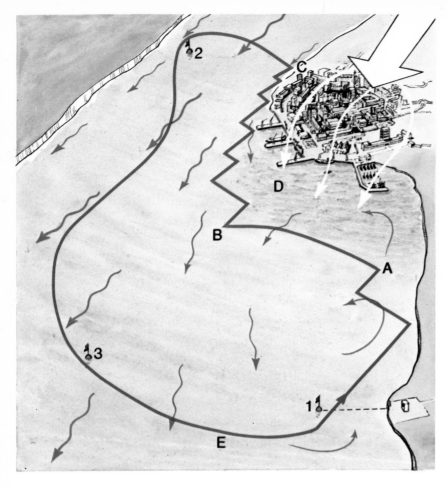

of a detour? Can one get close inshore to avoid a current or is the boat's draft too great? (0.7)

In any one race starting at any one time there will be only one theoretically fastest course (0.8). If all the navigational problems have been solved correctly and, in the absence of interference, then the boat taking this course must by definition win. To this extent it is a problem of boat-speed and navigation.

It is quite true to say that many a race has been won without the winner having ever come within sparring distance of another competitor. Though most frequently occurring in offshore races, it is by no means unknown for this to happen even on tight inshore small-boat courses, especially when a fast crew manages to get clear away at the start (0.9).

For the offshore crew there may be sufficient sense of satisfaction in outwitting the 'weather God' and solving the navigation and boat-speed problems, but there is no doubt that the regular runaway winner of a one-design dinghy series would begin to feel his victories to be somewhat hollow and lacking in the spice and thrill of good battles against equals. Annihilating the opposition is what we all say we want to do and is the result we strive for but, though a big win is most encouraging occasionally, the sense of achievement palls if done too frequently.

0.8 In this drawing are shown a number of features which can affect the theoretically fastest course, indicated here by the red line. The start, at buoy 1, is to windward and there is a favourable eddy close in towards the bank. The boat should tack close in until area A is reached when the influence of the buildings to windward will begin to be felt in disturbed air and alternate lulls and gusts (D).

So take a hitch across to area B, but not too far or the boat will reach the strongest part of the contrary current. Then make short tacks along the edge of the disturbed zone to C when buoy 2 can easily be fetched in a fast dash across the current.

Then move into the centre to pick up the best current to buoy 3. From there take the fastest course across the current to E and then luff up towards the finish.

0.9 The Danish Olympic Gold Medallist, Paul Elvstrom, gets clear away at the start of a Gold Cup race

0.10 100 Lasers wait for a World Championship start ▼

For most people in most races the perfect course can never be sailed simply because there are too many others all trying to do the same thing (0.10). So what happens when another boat comes close, interferes with one's chosen route, or even threatens collision? Who gives way? How does one even start without hitting somebody? And if a collision occurs, who pays for the damage? Well, of course, there are rules to cover almost every conceivable situation. The right-of-way rules can be very complicated but far too many people think of them as being solely for preventing imminent collisions. They are far more than this. They are the framework of a fascinating game, which is Yacht Racing, and which so many people never play—in fact so many actually refuse to play and do everything they can to avoid playing.

0.11 One-Tonners racing in the English Channel

0.12 Striving for top speed in 420 Class dinghies

But it is up to you whether you do play the whole game or only a part of it. Much depends on the type of boat being sailed and the sort of courses traditionally used by that class. Take care that the type of racing you choose to take part in gives the type of sport that you need.

The object of a sailing race, like most other races, is to get to the finishing line first. This is not quite true in the case of handicap races where one tries to beat the handicapper as well but, on the water, the feeling is the same—top speed and pass as many boats as possible!

Boats pass each other in several ways:

● *Superior boat-speed* Usually this is a small fraction of one per cent and in the absence of any other influence it can take many minutes for one boat to draw clear of another (0.11).

● *Superior techniques* This leads to greater boat-speed but can be far more dramatic than the minute improvement that better tuning can give. An example is slick crew-work in trimming sails to gusts and waves which can allow a boat to break through an opponent's wind-shadow with a sudden brief

surge (0.12). Planing is another example. Yet another is carrying the spinnaker on a reach in fresh winds when everyone else is broaching.

● *Interference with the wind supply* Backwind, foul air, lee-bowing, blanketing etc., are some of the common names for manoeuvres designed to interfere legally with the wind reaching the other boat (0.13). Obviously a partially interrupted wind supply is going to affect speed dramatically and so tactics leading to this are some of the most used and, for those at the receiving end, ones which immediate steps must be taken to avoid.

● *Tactics* This can be defined as the use of the rules to place others in bad positions or to improve ones own position. An example could be a boat which legally forces another to tack and end up in the wind-shadow of a third boat, or be pushed out into an unfavourable current. There are many other classic manoeuvres and we shall be looking at some later.

● *Navigation and orientation* Not only better large scale navigation on offshore races but steering accurate courses to marks on small-boat triangles can often win places. Under this heading would come the reading of weather signs in general and also in terms of local shifts, gusts and flat spots.

● *Gamesmanship and psychology* Distracting the other crew by one means or another, not only on the water, comes under this heading but one must always keep in mind the basic racing rule which says that a boat may only employ *fair sailing*, superior speed and skill in attempting to win (see appendix). However it would be hard to show that a crew gazing at the top of another boat's mast was employing unfair means, and yet the skipper might well think something was wrong up there so that his steering and concentration would be bound to suffer!

0.13 *These Solings are gybing and the leader has lost the wind in his spinnaker due to being blanketed by the boat behind*

● *Training and technique* There are other ways that a crew can cause a competitor to become rattled and to make mistakes. Superior training and perfection in technique and boat-handling will enable a crew to tack faster or to gybe without collapsing the spinnaker, not once but several times in succession if need be for example. Dinghy crews especially can benefit from physical training to enable them to hang out longer and harder (*0.14*).* Offshore crews too need endurance to last out their opponents in a long tough race. There have been many occasions of crews losing a certain win due to physical or mental collapse.

And so it can be seen that a yacht race encompasses a wide range of qualities, perhaps greater than in any other sport.

*See the bibliography at the end for further books specialising in these aspects of racing.

Let's go racing!

Before deciding on the level of racing that you think you would like to go for, why not get a brief idea of what is involved in actually taking part in a race?

Boats cannot be made to remain stopped on the water except when anchored or moored. Some races are occasionally started with all boats on the beach but nearly always a flying start method is used.

Unfortunately also, one cannot paint a starting grid on the sea and so a somewhat imaginary and vague start line has to be described to the competitors, usually as lying between two buoys or marks. A very great part of the skill of the race is in getting your boat to the best position on the line, travelling at top speed in the right direction, at exactly the moment that the start is signalled (0.15).

In fact, each race or group of races has to have a special set of *Sailing Instructions* which describes the starting and finishing lines and the course as well as many other technical points which may not be covered in the international *Racing Rules* themselves. Until you are familiar with all this it can be totally bewildering to be faced with a set of Sailing Instructions, let alone a rule book! It is the aim of this book to show how it all works and to lay the groundwork for your first win.

0.15   The start of a race

0.14   Physical fitness is a part of racing

The Course

The course runs from the starting line round a series of marks (0.16) to a finishing line. The identity of the marks will be given in the sailing instructions and you may have to refer to charts or course diagrams in order to identify them. You will also be told which way the marks have to be rounded and whether more than one circuit has to be completed.

0.16. Solings gybe round a mark

If possible, starts are made by arranging for the course from the starting line to the first mark to be dead to windward. This is best because it enables many boats to sail relatively unobstructed by others for the first and most congested part of the race, enabling the faster boats with the better crews to get to some extent clear of the bunch before the first turning mark is reached.

This does not mean that a boat which is well back has no chance of winning. On the contrary, there may be many opportunities to capitalise on the leader's mistakes or to make the most of differing wind or current conditions, or even by using better techniques and superior boat-speed to catch up and still take the winner's gun. But there can be no denying that a first class start and a well sailed first 'leg' is more than half the battle won.

The Start

The race is started by a series of warning signals, followed by a starting signal. Because the boats have no brakes and the starting line is not marked on the surface of the water, there is a considerable area of uncertainty about relative positions at the moment of the start (*0.17*). It is rare for more than a few boats to be within a yard or two of the line at the start and many may be some distance from it. Equally,

11

the wind is never constant so one part of the line may be more nearly to windward, and thus more sought-after, than another at any one moment.

It is obvious that a boat which is travelling at full speed just behind the line at the starting signal will have a big advantage over one which has arrived a little early and has had to slow down to avoid crossing too soon. Being over the line too early is disastrous in most cases since the erring boat has to return and restart in the face of a horde of boats going the other way (0.18). Hence it can be appreciated that there is not only a great deal of

skill but also a full measure of luck in making a near perfect start.

When you also take into account the close proximity of many other boats with keyed up crews all striving after the same perfect start, and the cut-up wind and water from multitudes of flapping sails and pounding hulls, it can readily be seen why starting raises the blood pressure and causes tempers to become short.

But, for the beginner, there is no need at all for anxiety because there is no compulsion to start at the most congested point, nor even to start at or immediately after the

signal. Why not get the feel of the game by starting a little late until confidence is gained and a few basic rules are learnt? Watch the others and see what they do.

A sailing race is surely the most involved type of sport in existence. It has been likened to chess but, though some moves have inevitable results which can be worked out in advance by a sufficiently clear-thinking and mathematical brain, there is far more to it than that.

Some world champions have indeed based their success on finely worked out mathematical analyses.

0.17 *The mast on the starting boat and the limit buoy are lined up to form the start line*

0.18 *One boat, on the right, has started too early and has to go back to re-start*

Others are strong and fit and wear down the opposition with their determination and stamina. Still others are experts at tuning their boats and hence can make up to some extent for deficiences in other departments. Some have the ability to gather a crew round them and weld them into a team with top efficiency in every job ranging from tactician to helmsman, navigator to sail-trimmer, foredeck hand to winch-grinder. Such a man is the essential catalyst which enables a whole crew to perform with superb cohesion.

There have been many champions who have been demonstrably weak in some department. Some are no good in light airs, some the opposite. Some win races on home ground and never abroad. Some are good starters and others good finishers. Some can exploit a close situation, others get rattled and make a mess of it. Some are accident prone under pressure or just plain careless. Some have intuitive flair but are not good at the nuts and bolts' and so their boats often fall to bits.

The first leg

This variety makes the game more interesting but there are things one can point to as being within everyone's control to a great extent and we should be foolish to neglect them if we hope to win. For example, immediately after a windward start there is no doubt at all that the biggest race loser is sailing in 'dirty-wind' or 'foul-air' (0.19). Get your wind clear at almost any cost. Get away from under that competitor who is interfering with your airflow as fast as you can.

This leads to the need for boat-speed. Remember, everyone else is anxious and worried, too, and they are *all* sailing their boats slower than they might. Because of this you have a chance to gain.

And then, don't forget to think ahead. Remember where you are in relation to the next mark. Many a race has been lost by over-standing and going too far. What about that wind-shift you were expecting? Are you on the right side of the course to benefit from it?

Another good principle is to avoid trouble. Keep clear of other boats. Do not always stand on your rights and, for example, force a boat to tack so that she ends up under your lee bow. She may then back-wind you and slow you down. Equally, do not tack to leeward of another boat since you cannot then tack again freely. In fact do not tack at all unless there is a good reason because you lose a length or two each time. All these points will be more fully discussed in Part Three.

To summarise these golden rules:

● Get your wind clear
● Go for boat-speed
● Think ahead
● Avoid trouble

0.19   34 is sailing in 'foul air' from 47. 78 has broken through into clear wind

Every race has its 'rabbits'. Races *need* rabbits. Any race is made up of perhaps five to ten per cent who will provide the winner (barring freaks), another fifty to seventy per cent of good competent sailors, most of whom have won races of a lesser standard than this one. The remainder are rabbits. Even Olympic races have them—perhaps an even higher percentage than ordinary class championships since many countries send competitors even though the class may be totally non-competitive at home.

So do not be afraid of being a beginner. Top sailors positively like having them in the fleet. It makes the fleet look bigger, and hence 'better', and they seldom cause trouble because they are left behind even before the start! Everyone knows that you have to begin somewhere and it is up to you to change from a 'rabbit' to a 'hare' as soon as possible—the first stage on the road to winning.

The first mark

So you finally arrive at that first windward mark and now you are at last racing against equals! The experts and the main body of the fleet have gone and are half way to the next mark. Two or three other boats are shaping up to round your mark with you and now is the time to start applying a few of the lessons you may have picked up from books or from crewing. We will not discuss technical details now, but you might be sufficiently in possession of your scattered wits to remember to come to the mark on the starboard tack, which gives you right of way, and also to make sure that you have not under-stood it so that you would have to tack again at an awkward moment (*0.20*). Did you forget the current? No? Good! So you bear away round the mark leaving one unfortunate boat who *did* forget, having to tack again and make another shot. One down—and twenty-five to go!

The second leg

Another boat is only just ahead of you. Can you catch him? You seem to be gaining. Perhaps he forgot to raise his centreboard. No—his crew is bailing! It must have been the boat you saw partly filled after a panic tack to avoid a starboard tack boat just before the mark (*0.21*).

You charge past him in a shower of spray. Two down and twenty-four to go! You are beginning to enjoy this. Where is the next one? There he is—and his crew is getting the spinnaker ready. Heavens! That means you have to do the same. Crew! Are you ready?

Amid frantic scrabbling you make sure that guy, sheet and halyard are clear while your crew clips on the sail corners and sets the pole in position. You have done this before many times on your own but this is the first time under pressure.

0.21 This swamped Fireball will get going again but has lost a lot of distance

0.20 The starboard tack boat only just manages to lay the windward mark

0.22   In this 505 balance is critical when hoisting the spinnaker

You cannot bear away to make it easier because of the course to the next mark. It just has to go up right first time (*0.22*). Take a deep breath. Hoist away. Cleat the halyard. Grab the guy. Call to the crew to sheet in the flogging sail and— bingo!—a perfect set. Hang on tight. You are away and planing fast.

Time to take a quick glance at the other boat—he's muffed his set and the sail is still flogging. With luck you will be up level before he gets going. Now it's neck and neck for the next mark (*0.23*). Surging on the waves you gain half a length then lose it time and again until finally the mark is reached. You can't remember the rules about 'overlaps' or 'two-length circles'. Better play safe. You are outside. He gybes inside you— gains four lengths in as many seconds and you are firmly back in twenty-fifth place again (*0.24*).

Oh well! You will know how important it is to get the inside position at a gybe mark next time!

The lee mark

The second reaching leg is a procession. You are well settled down now and so is the boat ahead. You cannot make any impression on him. But the lee mark is coming up. What if you hang on to your spin-

0.23   The reaching leg is a high-speed dash

the question comes 'When do we tack for the finishing line?' If you tack too soon you will have to tack again and he may not let you since he will have right of way being then on starboard tack. Better to over-stand a little, but not too much—remember the boat astern that could nip in ahead.

So you try to assess angles and speeds in your mind until finally you call 'lee-oh!' and round you go for the last effort.

You are getting tired and the other boat is now on your weather quarter looking good. He seems to be going faster. You can hear his bow smashing into the waves but you daren't look.

Squeeze up—give him some backwind—the line is only 100 yards away now but what about the angle? Is it square to the wind? Which end is nearer? You decide for the far end away from the com-

0.24   This 470 will lose several lengths by rounding outside

0.25   The spinnaker was dropped too late

naker a little longer and try to close the gap? (*0.25*)

He plays safe and you gain two lengths coming round the mark and sheeting in hard on the wind just behind him (*0.26*). Now what? Tack, or try to pinch out of his back-wind? You have already managed to gain half a length to windward of his course and so you try to squeeze another half a degree closer to the wind.

The final leg
Hike hard—sails in tight—boat upright—keep her moving—luff for that big wave—now bear off down its back. That's good. Now where is he? He's out of sight be-hind the jib—to leeward but still ahead. Watch him, crew, in case he tacks!

Slowly, slowly, inch by inch you gain. A test of nerves and muscle as well as boat tuning until finally

mittee boat and ease sheets slightly. He keeps pinching but catches the wind shadow from the committee boat and you scrape across the line a length ahead and are rewarded by a toot from a horn followed two seconds later by another toot for him (*0.27*).

You are exhausted but you and your crew feel marvelous. It was a tremendous battle and you won! No you didn't win the *other* race—the one for the experts—but you certainly won the race for rabbits! And there were three boats behind you!

And that is the best thing about yacht racing. Even within a race there are various levels. It is surprising how in a series you find that you come up against the same boats again and again. A great cameraderie develops at all levels. Eventually you work your way up to the top and then move on, if that is your ambition, to ever more demanding levels of racing, always meeting like minds but always in different conditions. No two races are ever the same.

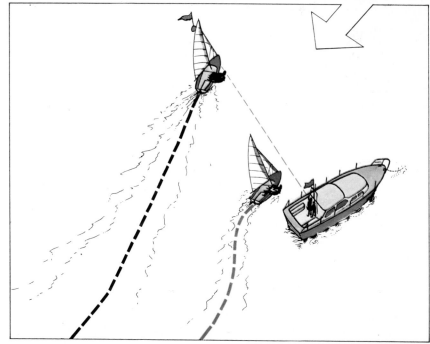

0.27 The finish

Part Two

The Background
to Winning

Chapter 1

The Psychology of Winning

Among the frantic chasing after newer and better boat designs, faster sails and the latest go-fast goodies, and after one has been brain-washed by the claims of advertisers and the sometimes ill-informed reports of news-hounds, it is easy to forget that the top boats in a class can all sail at the same speed and that the real differences lie in the use that is made of the motive power—which is, the variable, fickle and ungovernable wind.

The really valuable talent is to be able to guess better than the rest where and when the wind will blow. The really useful skill is to know how to place you boat to take advantage of every sort of situation.

Let us not denigrate fine tuning, expert technical skill and impeccable boat handling; all are important for success, as is the use of a boat which is competitive in design and well maintained. But the range of possibilities for winning races *without* requiring superior boat-speed is enormous.

There are some helmsmen who seem able to win races in spite of keeping out of the rat-race. They often come out top in a tactical duel leaving the loser to feel, wrongly, that his own boat is slow. They frequently appear in the lead after having what appears to be an amazing stroke of luck. They often end up as winners of a championship series without perhaps having won an individual race. Such helmsmen tend to earn an enviable and mystical reputation for winning and this tends to feed their success since opponents feel themselves half beaten before the start. They seem to combine incredible luck with only moderate boat-speed. It hardly seems to be fair!

These winners tend to be quiet and thinking people and the real reason for their outstanding results is just that—thinking ahead. It is the race as a game—a problem to be solved—which interests such helmsmen. It is not so much man against man but mind against mind which is the key to their success.

To be 'lucky' like this is not really magic and anyone can learn the secrets. If you want to win without being a super-fit fanatic with gorilla-like biceps you can do it. It only needs a study of the game as a whole and the cultivation of the correct mental approach to the problems. Don't allow emotion to influence you. Don't regard an inefficient committee, the complicated rules, the unstable wind, the tough competition as being against you. Search out their weak points, get to know some facts, use a little psychology and above all get into your head a desire and a will to win. Look for the ways in which you can turn the situation to your advantage.

Learn to be a winner

Do you recognise who this is (*1.1*)? It might be any one of thousands of young people doing something which can be seen any day at any sailing club—pulling his boat up the slip after a race. It could have been you or me or Joe Brown—but it was not! It is a portrait of one of the supreme winners of all time and he had just won his first Olympic Gold Medal, aged 19.

He was a skipper who had his failings like everyone else—he was very poor indeed in lighter winds, in those far off days of 1948—but he was absolutely determined to succeed. He never gave up and he conquered every set-back, winning World Championships in eight different international classes, once with a broken leg still strapped up.

Paul Elvstrom's story is an example of what anyone could still do, if they put their whole mind to winning. You may not want to be quite so all-conquering but, within the limits that you set yourself, there is no reason why anyone should not win races and go on winning.

So the surest way to improve your racing results is to cultivate the right mental attitude and to learn something about every aspect of the game. What follows here is the background knowledge which will enable anyone with a competitive boat and crew to win any race anywhere. This book does not go into immense and exhaustive detail but, from first-hand experience, it points the way and explains some of the race-winning ideas which have proved decisive time and again.

First we have to know something about the racing rules. Everybody hates them—but why? Get them on your side and you have a great weapon to aid you. In spite of the first paragraph of the next chapter they are not so difficult and you only need to be familiar with a few to win your first race.

1.1 One of the greatest 'winners' of all time—aged 19.

Chapter 2

The Basis of the Racing Rules

The racing rules jungle

It is generally believed that the Racing Rules are complicated, confusing in their layout and they are certainly understood only sketchily by most racing sailors. Yet they are the essential rules by which a sailing race is conducted. The vital decision which can win or lose the champion's crown can depend on a sound understanding of these rules together with instant recall of the correct (or best) move to make.

It is not too difficult to sit down at a table with the rule book in front of you and work out step by step the merits of an incident (though there are many pitfalls even with this!) but it is quite another matter

2.1 Whose right-of-way?

21

to be able to decide on an instant, in the midst of the cut and thrust of rounding a mark in a jam of other boats, who has right of way, who can press his advantage and who has to back off this time (*2.1*). A fraction of a second's delay in making up one's mind could mean a time-wasting avoiding manoeuvre which could finish one's chance of a good place or even mean disqualification.

Perhaps more important, unless the rules are understood and are respected, the racing will certainly degenerate into chaos. Different sailing areas have also been known to develop their own private simplifications or interpretations of the rules so that a crew travelling to foreign regattas, or even to distant parts of their own country, may find unexpected special rules or omissions to be the general practice there. To the strict rule observer this can be utterly demoralising; to the easy-going the racing at such a place may be totally unrewarding.

How many times have we seen competitors going away feeling sore because, although they have failed to observe the written rules and have been correctly protested against, they cannot accept their error. Equally, we have seen sailors trying hard to obey the rules but being unable to enforce them owing to some competitors, and even the race committee, failing to back them up when they protest. These people go away with a feeling of despair.

38.5	CURTAILING A LUFF The *windward yacht* shall not cause a *luff* to be curtailed because of her proximity to the *leeward yacht* unless an *obstruction*, a third yacht or other object restricts her ability to respond.
38.6	LUFFING TWO OR MORE YACHTS A yacht shall not *luff* unless she has the right to *luff* all yachts which would be affected by her *luff*, in which case they shall all respond even if an intervening yacht or yachts would not otherwise have the right to *luff*.
39	**Same Tack — Sailing Below a Proper Course after Starting** A yacht which is on a free leg of the course shall not sail below her *proper course* when she is clearly within three of her overall lengths of either a *leeward yacht* or a yacht *clear astern* which is steering a course to pass to leeward.
40	**Same Tack — Luffing before Starting** Before a right-of-way yacht has *started* and cleared the starting line, any *luff* on her part which causes another yacht to have to alter course to avoid a collision shall be carried out slowly and in such a way as to give a *windward yacht* room and opportunity to keep clear, but the *leeward yacht* shall not so *luff* above a *close-hauled* course, unless the helmsman of the *windward yacht* (sighting abeam from his normal station) is abaft the mainmast of the *leeward yacht*. Rules 38.4, (Hailing to Stop or Prevent a Luff); 38.5, (Curtailing a Luff); and 38.6, (Luffing Two or more Yachts), also apply.
41	**Changing Tack — Tacking and Gybing**
41.1	BASIC RULE A yacht which is either *tacking* or *gybing* shall keep clear of a yacht *on a tack*.
41.2	TRANSITIONAL A yacht shall neither *tack* nor *gybe* into a position which will give her right of way unless she does so far enough from a yacht *on a tack* to enable this yacht to keep clear without having to begin to alter her course until after the *tack* or *gybe* has been completed.
41.3	ONUS A yacht which *tacks* or *gybes* has the onus of satisfying the race committee that she completed her *tack* or *gybe* in accordance with rule 41.2.
41.4	WHEN SIMULTANEOUS When two yachts are both *tacking* or both *gybing* at the same time, the one on the other's *port* side shall keep clear.

SECTION C — Rules which apply at marks and obstructions and other exceptions to the Rules of Section B

When a rule of this section applies, to the extent to which it explicitly provides rights and obligations, it over-rides any conflicting rule of Section B, Principal Right of Way Rules and their Limitations except rule 35, (Limitations on Altering Course.

42	**Rounding or Passing Marks and Obstructions**
42.1	ROOM AT MARKS AND OBSTRUCTIONS WHEN OVERLAPPED When yachts are about to round or pass a *mark*, other than a starting *mark* surrounded by navigable water, on the same required side of an *obstruction* on the same side:
	(a) An outside yacht shall give each yacht *overlapping* her on the inside, room to round or pass the *mark* or *obstruction*, except as provided in rules 42.1(c), 42.1(d) and 42.4, (At a Starting Mark Surrounded by Navigable Water). Room includes room for an *overlapping* yacht to *tack* or *gybe* when either is an integral part of the rounding or passing manoeuvre.
	(b) When an inside yacht of two or more *overlapped* yachts either on opposite *tacks*, or on the same *tack* without *luffing* rights, will have to *gybe* in order most directly to assume a *proper course* to the next *mark*, she shall *gybe* at the first reasonable opportunity.
	(c) When two yachts on opposite *tacks* are on a beat or when one of them will have to *tack* either to round the *mark* or to avoid the *obstruction*, as between each other rule 42.1 shall not apply and they are subject to rules 36, (Opposite Tacks Basic Rule), and 41, (Changing Tack — Tacking or Gybing).
	(d) An outside *leeward yacht* with luffing rights may take an inside yacht to windward of a *mark* provided that she hails to that effect and begins to *luff* before she is within two of her overall lengths of the *mark* and provided that she also passes to windward of it.
42.2	CLEAR ASTERN AND CLEAR AHEAD IN THE VICINITY OF MARKS AND OBSTRUCTIONS When yachts are about to round or pass a *mark*, other than a starting *mark* surrounded by navigable water, on the same required side or an *obstruction* on the same side: (a) A yacht *clear astern* shall keep clear in anticipation of and during the rounding or passing manoeuvre when the yacht *clear ahead* remains on the same *tack* or *gybes*:

2.2   An example of the way the racing rules are phrased

The reason for these two extremes is, at least partly, the comprehensive complexity of the rules themselves. To the rule makers the wording is a model of clarity and, indeed, the phrasing and punctuation of the various clauses have been refined over the years to eliminate any hint of an ambiguous meaning (*2.2*). But there is no doubt at all that to the beginner (and, dare we say it, to the great majority of all racing sailors) the arrangement of the rules is confusing and full of traps. Some beginners are undoubtedly frightened away from ever starting to race their boats, while others play only half the game and still more ignore the rules altogether.

How then can these rules be explained in a way that gives the beginner a better chance and even the expert a vastly improved standard of performance?

2.3   An aquatint of 1842 shows a horrifying situation developing at the start!

Rules development

Let us begin by thinking of the rules as being devised by sailors and not by chairborne rule-makers. They arose because of the need to avoid expensive collisions, and the resulting law suits, between owners of big yachts in the infancy of yacht racing during the last century (*2.3*). They were first written down in 1875 and have developed and expanded by trial and error and under the influence of case-law ever since. They are still changing and being added to, sometimes very significantly, because the whole attitude to yacht racing is sharper and more professional today. But the basis mainly remains constant and only the details progress and inevitably become ever more involved as new incidents come to light necessitating yet more amendments.

And here lies our first hope of simplification because the principles are still the same as they have always been and the fundamental rules are also well and truly based. The real complication comes in a whole host of exceptions and special cases. Many of these are pretty obscure but some of them crop up time and time again.

Secondly the order and arrangement of the present rules bears little relationship to what actually happens on the water. So let us consider them more logically, not by clauses and sub-clauses, paragraphs and sub-paragraphs, but as part of a race which has a start, a middle and a finish.

Of course, we shall never be able to cover every exception and special case in this way. Indeed, it is perfectly feasible for a sailor to race for years only knowing and using two or three basic rules, but to get the most fun from the sport the rules should be studied in detail and so we will do this in Part Three and at the same time discuss the tactics which stem from them. The Rules will be listed in the Appendix and cross-referenced in the text. The actual rules as authorised by the IYRU will always have to be the last resort in case of dispute.

What a boat can do and cannot do in any situation is governed by the right-of-way rules, which are found in the IYRU Rule Book*, and what the keen crew really needs to know is how to use these rules to improve his boat's position—to pass the boats ahead—to win the race. Inter-boat tactics are totally dependent on the way the rules are framed. Therefore we shall be dealing with the conduct of a typical race in a tactical way from the individual boat's viewpoint in Part Three and the rules should then fall into place naturally.

Basic principles

In yacht racing there are some basic principles of a general nature which govern how the game is to be played. They are often forgotten and are frequently not well understood. The most fundamental might be stated as giving the other boat a *fair deal*. One aspect of this is what the Rules call *fair sailing*. It means that, only wind power is to be used to propel the boat. It also says that racing is an individual sport and so no teaming up against another competitor is allowed. Specially organised inter-team racing is almost a different sport but uses the same rules, with some additions and exceptions.

Fair sailing also forbids the use of manual power to move the boat. This is called *unfair propulsion* and obviously paddling would be a clear cut violation of this. So would sculling with the rudder but other

actions are not so clear. For example roll-tacking is accepted even though in little wind it certainly propels the boat (*2.4 & 2.5*). It is up to the other competitors to object if they think a boat is roll-tacking excessively. Similarly, gybing violently can give a shove, and there are other ways such as rocking the boat when running, as well as fanning the sails and pumping the sheets. Some of these actions are effective in all wind strengths, others being mainly light-air techniques.

Obviously a crew has to work hard physically to trim the sheets, sail the boat and keep it in balance. The dividing line between fair and unfair sailing comes where the crews' actions would propel the boat in the absence of wind. Strictly, one roll-tack or other action would come in this category. However this is accepted as being legal, but more than once or perhaps twice in a short time would not.

This leads on to a principle which is seldom understood and causes a great deal of trouble. The right-of-way rules deal with situations when boats meet so that one of them has to do something to avoid touching. There are necessary limits within which the rules operate. For example an over-taking boat has to keep clear until the moment that it overlaps the boat ahead. At this moment another set of conditions starts to apply and the right-of-way may change.

There is thus always a change-over point when one situation ends and a new one begins. The principle to remember is that the boat which becomes obliged to take some avoiding action does not have to *begin* to do so until the change-over point actually occurs. In other words a boat need not anticipate a new situation and has to be given *time to respond.*

The next principle leads on from this. If a boat manoeuvres into a position which gives it right-of-way over another, the *onus of proof* that it did so correctly within the limits of the rules and that enough time was given for the other to respond rests with the boat taking the action. Sometimes there are two possible answers in a rapidly changing set of conditions and then the one taking the first action has to do the proving though it is possible that both may in fact be wrong.

Equally, it is only fair that a boat should *hail* another when she is going to make a sudden manoeuvre which will give her right-of-way, such as a tack, which may not be foreseen by another boat.

And this again leads to manoeuvres designed to *prevent* a right-of-way boat from keeping clear or *balk* her when trying to do so. These manoeuvres are not fair sailing and come under *restrictions on altering course*.

And this leads on to actual *collisions*. The principles of seaman-

*See Appendix for addresses and details.

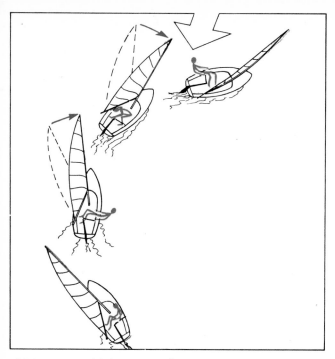

ship are to avoid danger at all costs. Therefore, for a true seaman, sailing in close proximity to another is wrong. Also sailing close to a shoal or a mark is wrong. In racing these things happen all the time and in fact the whole essence of a yacht race is that 'a miss is as good as a mile' when it comes to upholding your rights or cutting a turning mark as fine as possible (2.6). But danger and damage must be minimised and so collisions are discouraged. Unfortunately, actual contact between boats is sometimes the only way of establishing the facts of a situation but, if deliberate, it has to be comparatively gentle contact. The right-of-way boat will find herself penalised as well as the other if the damage is more than superficial.

2.4 & 2.5 The roll-tack. The helmsman leans sharply outboard, pulling the sail to windward, and at the same time he puts the rudder over to start the tack. When the boat is heeling to windward, still being pulled forward by the airflow created by the initial heave, he moves to the other side and straightens the tiller. The sail should remain full until the boat is on its new close-hauled course, when it flips across to the new tack.

The boat in the photo has just reached the final stage.

It is often hard to decide whether such action is fair or unfair propulsion (see text, opposite page).

Of course, obstructing another boat by trying to pass to windward, by *luffing* is not always successful. Nor is the wind-shadow enough to stop a determined and clever crew, who can time a gust or a wave just right to enable their boat to surge through to leeward (*2.8*). But the leader has a considerable advantage in defence when boats are on the same tack and the wind is ahead of the beam.

But the wind is not always ahead of the beam and courses are very seldom arranged as straight legs from A to B. Almost always they are variations of a closed circuit, often with two or more laps. This immediately gives enormous opportunities for place changing since the course contains many different points of sailing and there are a number of marks to round as well as differing wind, wave and current conditions on the course as a whole. Because of this, the possibilities of boats meeting, crossing or converging, rather than simply overhauling one another, multiply greatly and hence the rules to cover what each boat has to do get rather more elaborate.

Basically the principle about the leading boat being able to defend only applies if both boats are sailing parallel or nearly so and on the

Basic Right-of-Way Rules

The rules of the game can be thought of as achieving several ends and the avoidance of imminent collisions is only one of them. One of the chief principles of the rules is that a leading boat which is threatened with being passed is enabled to defend its position within limits. Thus, if two boats are sailing on the same tack (i.e. booms on the same sides) the leader may obstruct the overtaker from passing to windward by altering course to try to hit her. This is called *luffing* (*2.7-A*). However, it is thought sufficient for the leader's wind-shadow (dirty wind or foul air) (*2.7-B*) to defend her against a boat overtaking to leeward and she must not obstruct her further by bearing away.

▼ 2.7

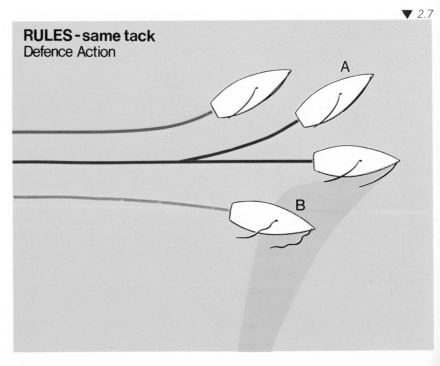

RULES - same tack
Defence Action

can luff her if she tries to pass to windward and even hit her if she can but, the Windward/Leeward rule still applies to prevent her from bearing away to touch a boat overtaking to leeward. It is only when meeting on opposite tacks that the challenger has the same rights as the leader, namely—whichever boat is on Port tack has to give way.

When *running* the leader has no advantage. Indeed, it is the over-taker who can now interfere with the wind supply and can draw up level without great difficulty. The leader can still luff but the important tactical manoeuvre on this point of sailing is to overlap the leader at the leeward turning mark and this is difficult for the leader to prevent.

same tack the basic rule is:

● *Windward boat (Red) gives way to Leeward boat (2.9)*

If one boat is close-hauled and the other sailing free and there is risk of a collision, the one sailing freer is considered to be the more windward boat for the purpose of this rule (see lower drawing).

When boats are on opposite tacks (main booms on opposite sides) there is a second basic rule.

● *Port tack (Red) gives way to Starboard tack (2.10)*

When sailing on a leg which is to *windward* (i.e. at some point on the leg boats will have to change tacks to reach the next mark) the leading boat also has another advantage. She can cover all the movements of an attacking boat and can slow her down by interfering with her wind supply. She

2.9 ▼

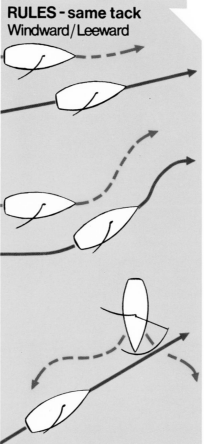

RULES - same tack
Windward / Leeward

▼ 2.10

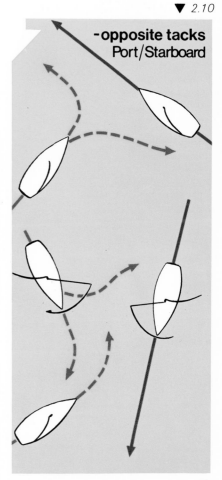

- opposite tacks
Port / Starboard

An *overlap* occurs when some part of the boat is ahead of a line at right angles to the aftermost part of the boat ahead—the 'transom line (*2.11*). At A an overlap is about to start.

If a boat is overtaking another and they are both on the same tack it is obvious that the Windward/Leeward rule cannot apply until the overtaker makes a move to go one side or the other (*B or C*). It is laid down therefore that the *overtaker keeps clear* until the Windward/Leeward rule begins to apply. At B Black can luff to try to prevent Red passing. At C Black is not allowed to bear away (see also page 120).

At any time when racing a boat may have to alter course to avoid some *obstruction* or to *round a mark*. The basic principle is that a boat which is *inside* another (i.e. is overlapping the other on the side nearest the obstruction or mark) can claim room to pass it on the same side. She cannot normally be squeezed out (*2.11-D & 2.12*).

Remember too that an obstruction does not have to be stationary. It can be another boat or ship including another boat in the same race, particularly one with right-of-way or which is temporarily disabled or capsized, for example. (*11.37*).

The reason for this is mainly safety but more places are won and lost at marks and obstructions than anywhere else except at the start itself, and the full rules covering all the possible variations are long and involved. The reader is referred to the IYRU Rules themselves and various specialised books dealing with their introduction which are listed in the Bibliography.

If these simple basic rules and principles are understood they will go a long way towards enabling anyone to get out and race their boat successfully and crews should certainly now begin to know instinctively whether a particular manoeuvre is allowable or not. Our conscience can often tell us the answer.

▼ *2.11*

RULES
Overlaps
Overtaking

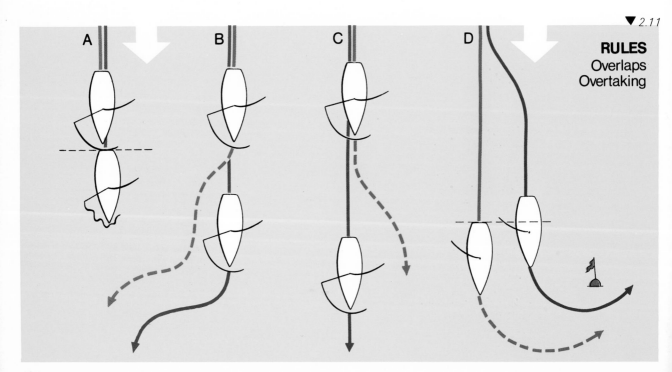

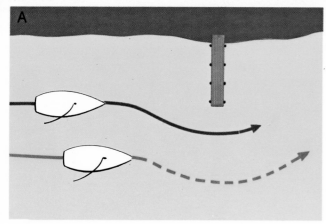

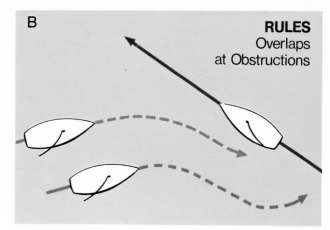

2.12 ▲

Where the rules break down

The standard of rule observance and the general *feeling* during racing varies markedly from class to class. It may have something to do with the people at the top of each class and their personal attitudes to racing.

Among many top sailors there has evolved a sort of unwritten code which tacitly allows certain types of incident to pass unchallenged, which would infringe the rules if applied strictly, whereas others are totally unacceptable. In the classes I have raced this code usually divides the accidental minor infringement due to a genuine error of judgement (not ignorance) from an infringement resulting from a deliberate tactical manoeuvre which went wrong. In the latter case the offender was expected to take the penalty without question. He always knew and so did his opponent.

However, this occasionally resulted in generally slack respect for the rules and quite major pile-ups could occur at turning marks or on starting lines when no-one retired at all. Obviously someone was at fault and the chain reaction caused many boats to collide. No-one could possibly remember the relative positions of the boats even if they knew who they were. It would have been a waste of time to have had a full scale 'protest' meeting over the incident and so the matter was ignored, a fact that the conscientious observer found to be quite wrong.

Turning marks are common places where collisions occur and often no-one is afterwards sure who was right and who was wrong. There is no time to note witnesses and so the incident often passes without a culprit being found let alone being penalised. This is often unfair on the boat which had tried the right tactics and was denied the advantage that should have been hers.

The way to deal with these

will also impress on your neighbour the relative position of your two boats at a certain moment and this could be very valuable in establishing facts should an incident end in a protest hearing later (see chapter 14). Do not leave the shouting to the last moment when everyone is excited and confused.

This brief discussion on the *principles* of the rules is intended to put the reader in the right frame of mind to make the most of the tactics that are available within the rules of the sport.

The Rules Appendix gives further and more detailed information and also shows how the rules can be studied in detail. Cross-references are linked to every mention of the rules within the text and to every relevant illustration.

Part Three of this book shows how the rules are used to develop boat-to-boat tactics on the race course.

seemingly impossible situations is really quite simple but it needs everyone to have a good basic knowledge of the rules, and it also means *forethought* and *experience*.

Forethought, or thinking ahead, means that crews should learn to anticipate what is going to happen. It means that well before the gybe mark, for example, you should establish your rights and manoeuvre for position. As you approach a certain congestion point like this make sure that all the boats outside you know that you may need room. That means persuading your next door neighbours to pass on the message good and loud to the outsiders. Do not be afraid of making sure that everyone in range knows that you are going to insist on your rights.

This is also the time to note who is near you. A friendly exchange

Chapter 3

Prepare to Win

3.1   A 470 class championship race

to-boat tactics, which are covered in Part Three, in this and following chapters we enlarge on race strategy and the tactics which stem from external sources such as the weather and even from the Race Committee. These are much neglected but vital skills and as we shall see they overlap in some respects.

A plan of the course area

By this is not meant a little sketch of the way the marks are to be rounded as is found in many Sailing Instructions. This is of course essential too but I mean that you should also study a proper chart or map of the area including the land surrounding the course (*3.3*). A mental picture should be built up of the whole area 'from the air' and one should also try to picture what it will look like from sea level. Get some photographs too if possible so that you have some idea of the local features.

3.4 Code flag identifies the boat's class

Race Strategy

Races range in importance from a mid-week evening club handicap race for a dozen boats of mixed classes (*3.2*) to a full-scale world championship on open sea with all the paraphernalia of committee boats, jury, rescue services and spectators (*3.1*).

For the first the club will have a standard set of *Sailing Instructions* pinned to the club notice board and the course may be a fixed one. Variations are almost unheard of and the competitors know the instructions by heart and follow them almost automatically.

Championship races obviously will repay the utmost care in preparation, not only of the boat and

crew (which is not the subject of this book) but in the way the event is approached and the gaining of special knowledge to do with that race.

The advice which follows gives some of the essentials to success in a big race. Some of the advice is of limited use to the local club sailor but anyone with a desire to win will race away from home sometime and this is where careful planning pays off best.

In this book we assume that your boat measures correctly, is well prepared and in perfect tune for the conditions, your crew is well drilled and your handling techniques are sound, but more than this is needed for winning races. Apart from boat-

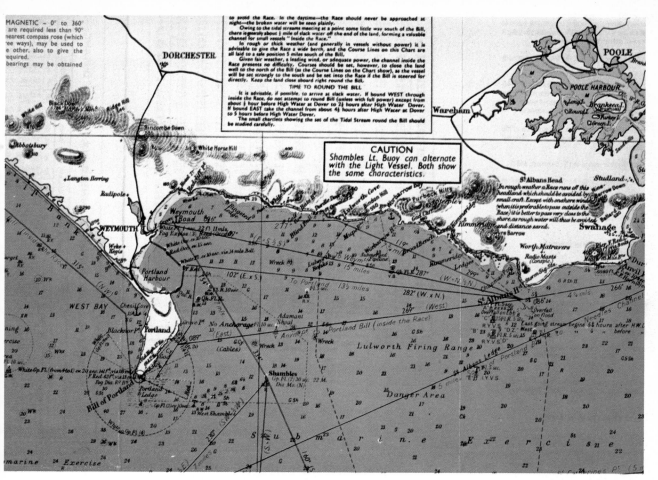

3.3 *A chart of the course area which shows local topography as well as features on the water*

Familiarity with the area means that you are less likely to get 'lost' and that you can exploit tactical situations without fear of going off course by overstanding the weather mark, for example. There are other reasons for this map study which will become clear shortly.

Special requirements

The Sailing Instructions are not always available in advance, so when you eventually get them it is vital to allow undisturbed time to go through them very carefully indeed.

Often there are special requirements which can range from having to fly an identifying Code Flag (3.4) to the alternative penalties, if any, which will apply during the race. There is an enormous range of possible things that the Race Committee may want to tell you and it should all be in the Sailing Instructions including course details, times of start, tidal information etc. It sometimes also happens that there is a mistake or ambiguity in the instructions. Clarify this before the race. Afterwards is too late.

Many a race has been lost, and not a few have been won, on account of the care with which the instructions have been studied.

Tactical equipment

We will be discussing in the next chapters the types of local knowledge that can easily be acquired by any competitor even at long distance. We shall then apply this knowledge to the smaller scale of certain parts of the course but first we need some basic equipment.

All boats need:

● A watch
● Note-board and wax pencils
● Compass
● Sailing instructions for the race
● Protest flag

Large boats can additionally have:

● Hand-bearing compass
● Charts and instruments
● Tide tables and pilotage books
● Tacking lines or marks on the deck

Watch (*3.5*) This can be either a stopwatch or one with a sweep second-hand. If the latter, the actual time of the warning signal should be entered on the note-board. It is easy to make a one minute error in timing.

The helmsman can take the time and if so the watch should be on his right wrist which will be easier to see when starting on starboard tack. In larger boats it is best for the crew or tactician to call out the final minute or two at ten second intervals. The only disdavantage to this is that it tells everyone round you the exact timing also.

Note-board and grease pencils (*3.6*). The board can be a piece of plastic, hand held in a larger boat, or it can be taped to the aft deck or side decks in a small boat. Even the surface of the decks themselves can be used for jotting down information with wax pencil (*5.21*). Some form of course calculator is also invaluable (see also Chapter 7).

3.5 A special watch which counts the time left before the start

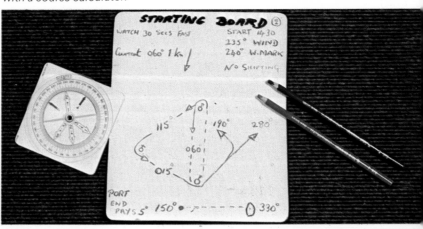

3.6 A note-board and grease pencils with a course calculator.

Compass. Either one compass on the centreline (*3.7*) or a matched pair immediately forward of the helmsman or the crew (*3.8*) can be fitted. In the case of the former the tactician or helmsman cannot see the central lubber's line when sitting outboard and so additional lines must be put on. This may lead to confusion in tense situations, such as the start, since the reading must be corrected.

For the same reason the special tactical compasses with moveable grids and coloured sectors may not be such a good idea. Above all it is wise to keep everything simple (see also *5.21* and Chapter 7).

A pair of compasses are easy to read but they must be matched and properly adjusted by an expert so that they read the same on all headings. They are also prone to magnetic error from knives in the pocket of a crewman sitting nearby or even from tins of soup on the galley shelf immediately below (*3.9*).

In a centreboard boat the compass need be only partially gimballed but in keel-boats it should swing freely at up to 40° of heel at least. The card should also be as nearly deadbeat as possible which can be tested in the shop to see how quickly it becomes stationary after being swung. Nothing is more frustrating to the tactician than a card which swings about at the least disturbance.

3.7   A centre-line compass with extra tacking lines

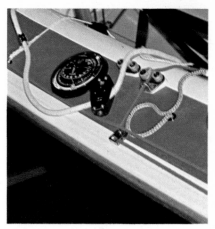

3.8   One of a pair of side-deck compasses with moveable grids

3.9 ▼

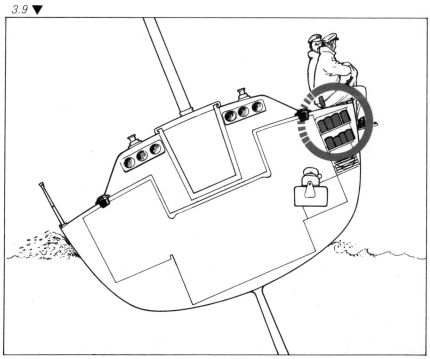

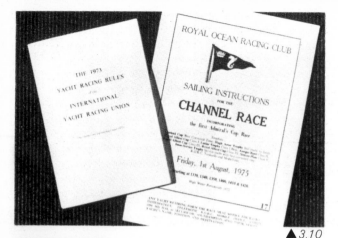

▲ 3.10

▲ 3.11

◀ 3.12

Sailing instructions and rule book (*3.10*). Together they contain all the rules under which the race is being run including any special requirements. They should have been studied in advance but will be needed on board in times of doubt.

Protest flag (*3.11*). If an incident occurs in which you think you have been wronged or if you hit another boat or a mark and you think it was not your fault you have to follow the rules for making 'Protests'. These include putting a flag in the rigging, usually Flag B which is a red swallow-tail flag (see also Chapter 14).

Sometimes there are alternative penalties to an infringement which can be accepted on the spot by showing a special flag. This should be carried if the instructions say so.

Hand-bearing compass (*3.12*). In larger boats this is almost essential. Get a good one. It is used not only for normal navigation purposes but it is much the best way of fixing the angle of the starting line, the proximity of the lay-lines when approaching the windward mark, and the relative positions, and hence change in positions, of other boats.

Charts and instruments. Boats large enough to fit chart tables should have a full set of charts for the area and plotting instruments well fastened down. In rough con-

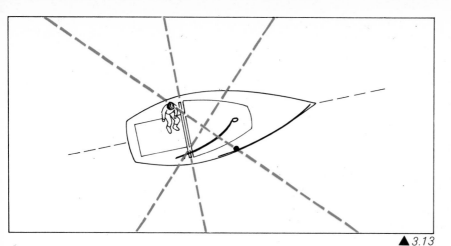

ditions everything flies about and may have to be retrieved from the oily bilge under the engine. Smaller boats can only use charts fixed into a portable transparent cover. All plotting has to be done beforehand with variations from the planned course entered on the noteboard during the race.

Tide tables and pilotage books. Mark the relevant pages beforehand and put them in a safe place. In a square, deep plastic bucket securely fastened down is one good method.

Tacking lines (3.13 & 3.14). Mark on the deck a line abeam and two lines 45° ahead and astern on both sides. Experience will tell you when to tack to lay a mark (beam line), when you can tack to cross a boat on the weather quarter (after line), and when you can cross a boat approaching on the opposite tack (forward line).

The actual angles will vary in different conditions but they provide a firm reference to start from. If you do not want to paint lines on the deck, the mainsheet track may provide a good reference abeam and you may be able to use a winch barrel or lee shroud as a sighting mark for the others.

The way the equipment is used will become clear as we discuss tactics and the race in detail.

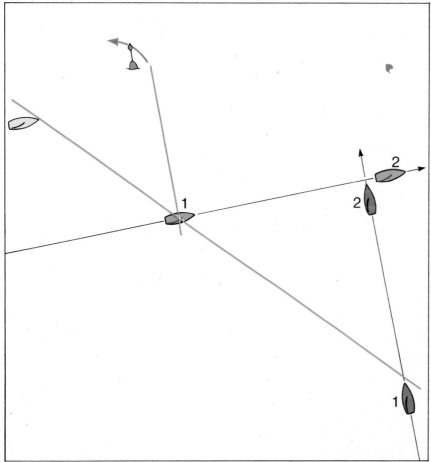

◄ 3.14

Chapter 4

Wind, Weather, Waves and Current

It sometimes happens that pure boat-speed will be enough to win the race. Even in one-design classes it is possible to tune and prepare the boat to such a pitch that, at least in some conditions, it can be sailed a fraction faster than the others. Given a good start and a steady wind this boat is bound to win. But it does not often happen like that. The wind is seldom steady and frequently a demonstrably

4.1   To sail, one needs wind!

faster boat does not win. Sometimes a very slow boat wins. In handicap races one often sees a smaller boat right up with the larger, faster leaders. How is it done? Is it luck?

Apart from better design, better tuning and better handling it can also be on account of better strategy, better tactics and the sort of preparation that eliminates, as far as possible, chance.

Weather Information
After all the preparation, measuring, gamesmanship and studying of rules have been done, we are in the end obliged to rely on the uncertainties of wind to propel our boats round the course (*4.1*).

The weather forecasts should therefore not be neglected and they must be treated for what they are, which is an overall summary of the large-scale weather as applied to the country as a whole. The local weather at your particular place may be very different, par-

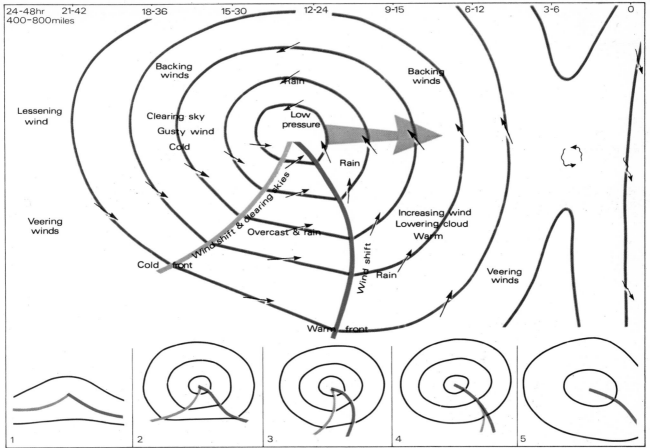

Lessening
wind

Backing
winds

Backing
winds

Clearing sky
Gusty wind
Cold

Rain

Low
pressure

Rain

Veering
winds

Wind shift & clearing skies

Overcast & rain

Increasing wind
Lowering cloud
Warm

Cold   front

Wind shift

Rain

Veering
winds

Warm   front

| 1 | 2 | 3 | 4 | 5 |

4.2   A typical advancing low pressure system in the Northern Hemisphere:
1   The system begins with a ripple wave
2   Developing and deepening
3   Maximum intensity
4   Starting to fill up
5   Nearly occluded

ticularly as regards wind speed and direction, but this does not mean that you should ignore the forecasts.

The information that you must obtain from the forecast or from the local Met Office, if any, is:

1 The overall situation; for example the existence of a stationary high pressure system, a depression approaching, passing to the South, passing to the North, receding or filling.

2 The imminent approach of warm or cold fronts and their time of arrival at your location.

3 The expected gradient wind, i.e. that caused by large weather systems as opposed to local heating.

4 Expected wind-shifts.

5 Possibilities of thunder storms.

6 Whether the isobars are curving so that they are concave on the side facing high pressure or that

facing low pressure. This information is vital for coastal sailing because, if the former the skies will be misty or mainly clear; if the latter they will be cloudy or overcast. The presence or otherwise of sun has a profound effect on local wind.

39

4.3 The edge of an advancing warm front beginning to cover seabreeze cumulus which will die out as the sun is cut off

4.4 Typical unstable clouds found in the period after a cold front. Thundery centres are building up

A point to note here is that Beaufort force, as given in forecasts, is an *average* speed. It is quite wrong, and technically meaningless, to talk about 'gusting to force 6'. Sailors often mis-interpret weather forecasts as a result of this. The gusting of a wind depends on the type of air stream and perhaps other features such as the presence of thunderstorms. Gusts can sometimes double (and lulls can halve) the mean wind force and so the likely amount of gusting should be *added* to the forecasted average wind.

With this information you now have to study the sky for yourself and perhaps also ask local advice.

From your own knowledge or from books on the weather you should know how the winds shift round a depression. A brief summary is given (4.2)—and what the sky may look like (4.3, 4.4, 5.2, 5.4). To check the position of low pressure, and hence the centre of a depression, stand with your back to the gradient wind (face the wind in the Southern Hemisphere). *Low* pressure will be on your *Left*.

The wind in advance of fronts, when the sky is overcast, tends to be steady. During the clearing skies after a cold front it is often very gusty. Winds off the sea tend to be steady. Off the land—gusty. In thundery conditions watch for the storm centres. The winds can be violent near them though their directions can often be predicted (see 'Clouds and Gusting Winds', page 55 *et seq*).

It nearly always pays to carry the correct sails for the lighter winds expected and then spill wind through the squalls. If the time scale and the size of boat allows it, extra sails can be carried and the rig changed as often as necessary but this is seldom possible in small boats. Flat sails in light winds are real race-losers, whereas the technique of carrying full sails temporarily in squalls can be learnt (see bibliography).

Local wind effects

Having built up a basic picture of the overall weather you must study the local topography and relate the two. This is where we have to go back to the map and think about the seabreeze and other thermal winds.

The basic rule is that air rises over a warm surface and so this air has to be replaced at the surface by new air coming in from the side. Obviously this new air comes from a cooler surface and it is then heated in its turn and the process repeats itself (4.5).

The second basic rule is that land both cools and heats faster than water. Thus land is usually cooler than water at night because it loses heat faster, and is warmer in the daytime under the influence of sun (4.6).

Thirdly, land sloping towards the sun heats faster than the land sloping away. So thermal winds are stronger and start earlier on South facing coasts (Northern hemisphere) and on the North sides of lakes in mountainous or hilly country (4.7).

4.5 ▲

4.6 ▲

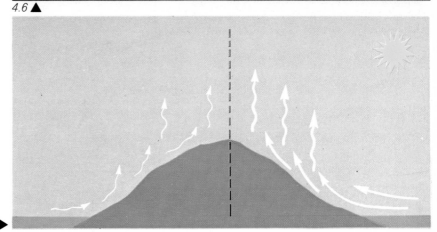

4.7 ▶

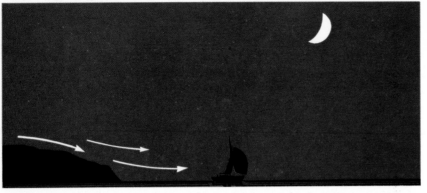

Seabreeze

The seabreeze is found to a greater or lesser extent on almost every coast but its influence varies widely,

- It prefers a coast with a flat hinterland.
- It does not like crossing ranges of hills and it will always funnel through even the shallowest of gaps (seabreeze windows).
- It is stronger on South facing coasts (Northern Hemisphere).
- It starts earlier in the day on East facing coasts and latest on West facing coasts.
- It can be steered by a river valley, estuaries, islands etc. at up to almost ninety degrees from its basic direction.
- Its direction is affected by the rotation of the earth.
- It superimposes itself on the prevailing gradient wind and thus it can often show as a *reduction* in strength of a stronger prevailing wind which opposes it or a shift in direction of a prevailing wind at other angles.
- It is weak or non-existent in cold seasons and strongest in the summer but on some hot days it may not be able to break through if there is a temperature inversion present (ask the local Met. service).

Seabreeze starts on or near the beach and, in simplest and most clear-cut form (i.e. no gradient wind) works against light offshore night wind (thermally induced by land being cooler than sea), caus-

ing it to die to a fitful calm during the morning, to be replaced by an increasing seabreeze (4.8) reaching a maximum in mid afternoon and then dying again, often quite suddenly.

It is important to visualise exactly what is happening (4.9) because races often take place in the seabreeze zone and the effects can be dramatic. I once was tactician aboard a yacht in a world championship series which we won

eventually by less than three points. We gained eight points in the last stages of one of the races during the series by correctly recognising an imminent collapse of the seabreeze and by taking appropriate action.

This particular example was very marked and had far reaching effects. The same types of place changes, in less dramatic form, are constantly occuring in races and the reasons are frequently un-

recognised and put down to luck. With experience you will realise that some people are always 'lucky'!

In the classic seabreeze situation the heated air over the land rises and is replaced by cooler air from the sea which then rises in its turn. The risen air meets the prevailing or night breeze higher up, is returned seawards where it cools again and drops to the surface to repeat the process continuously (4.9—top).

4.9 ▼

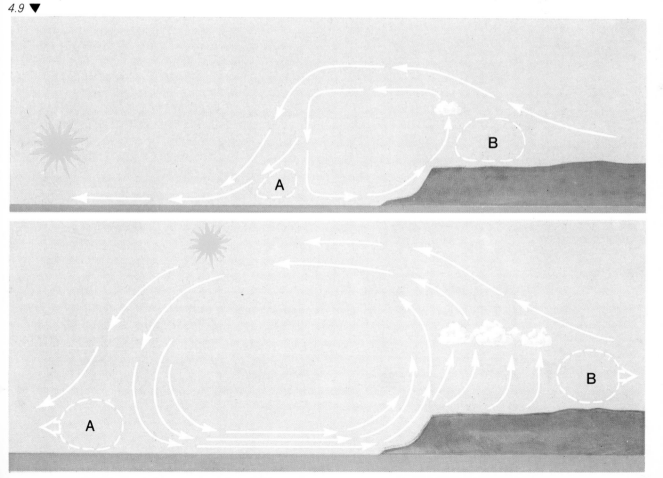

Where the descending air reaches the surface is a calm zone caused by the divergence of part going landwards to feed the seabreeze and part going seawards as the prevailing wind (A). There is also a similar 'seabreeze front' on the inland side where air is rising but here the surface winds are blowing towards the calm strip (B).

As the land heats up, a greater quantity of air is needed and so air is drawn in from further out to sea and moves in faster. The calm zone therefore starts near the beach and gradually moves seawards as the seabreeze increases, possibly reaching as far as two to ten miles out. The inland calm zone also moves inland and can reach as much as 40 miles from the coast on a good seabreeze day (4.9— lower).

Yacht racing, even offshore racing, is frequently held within a narrow strip of sea near the coast and there are often lakes and estuaries which are used for sailing within the influence of the landward area. It is obviously vital to know whether the wind is going to die or to shift 180 degrees or if it will increase from Force 1 to Force 4 within the next hour, for example— all typical occurrences in seabreeze conditions.

◀ 4.11   The seabreeze is imminent. Note the sharp cut-off in cloud over the coast line

The signs of seabreeze effects are clear skies over the coastal strip early (to allow the sun to heat the land) with developing cumulus cloud as the day progresses (showing that air is rising), clear skies at sea in the coastal zone showing that air is falling (*4.10, 4.11*). Often cumulus can be seen advancing seawards on the prevailing upper wind only to die away over the sea as it drops to feed the seabreeze.

Remember, cumulus may look to be very dense inland viewed from seaward but it usually has quite large gaps through which the sun can do its work. Upper cloud, often in advance of a front (*4.3*), or sheet cloud of any sort at any level (*5.2*) usually prevents a seabreeze from operating.

Remember also that the sea-breeze effect does not always show itself in this classic form. Less easy to recognise and less dramatic but, for this reason at least as worth-while to understand, is the combination of seabreeze and gradient wind (*4.12*).

All that is required is enough sun to heat the coastal land zone which shows, as before, in clear skies tending to develop cumulus cloud. Then you can assume that the sea-breeze is starting. If there is a pre-vailing gradient wind, rather than a thermally induced night breeze, the seabreeze will gradually start to modify this as its power increases.

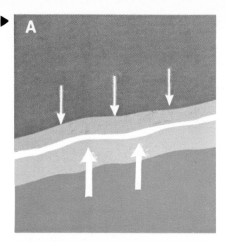

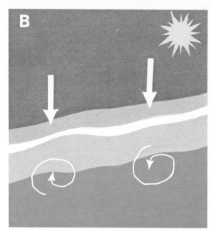

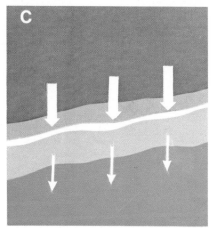

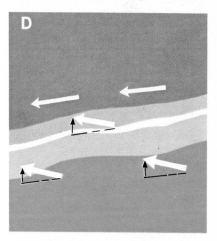

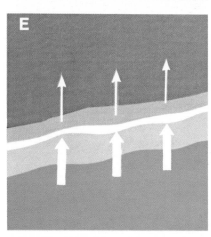

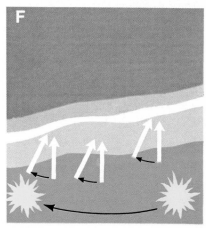

So watch out for the following effects (4.12):

A Light landbreeze dies and is replaced by seabreeze during the morning (classic case).

B Moderate landbreeze dies, becomes fitful with 180 degree swings and then returns in late afternoon.

C Fresh landbreeze reduces in strength during the day, returning to full strength in the evening (viz. mistral in Golfe du Lion).

D Wind parallel to the coast shifts gradually more onshore with the advance of the day. Easterly prevailing winds tend also to decrease, Westerlies to increase in both hemispheres.

E Onshore wind increases with the advance of the day.

F Gradient wind, when influenced by seabreeze, tends to shift during the day in the same direction as the sun. Particularly marked on a South facing coast (North facing in the Southern hemisphere) it is the reason why it so often pays to use the starboard side of a windward leg (port side in Southern Hemisphere).

Inland Winds

Very large lakes can have thermal wind patterns similar to seabreeze with air drawn shorewards during the day by the warmer land and being fed by sinking air over the centre of the lake. Visible signs of this are clear skies over the lake (sinking air—A) and cumulus over the land (rising air—B) (4.13).

▲ 4.13

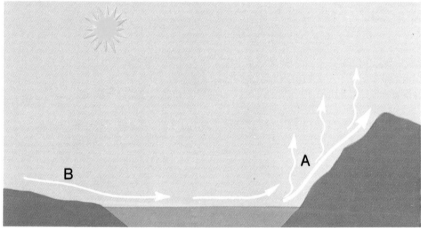

▲ 4.14

On smaller lakes it often pays to keep clear of the central area though the local topography has a much greater influence on the thermal wind pattern. For example, a lake with a mountainous Northern shore facing the South will generate anabatic winds (going up the slopes—A) as the sun heats the mountain sides (4.14). If the South shores are relatively low the air feed will come from there leading to a strong Southerly wind (B).

As in the case of seabreeze the effects of local heating can completely overwhelm the prevailing gradient wind. The thermal effect of a mountain side exposed to full sun can be very marked and when coupled with nearby slopes in deep shade can lead to very strong winds—anabatics going up heated slopes and katabatics descending cold slopes.

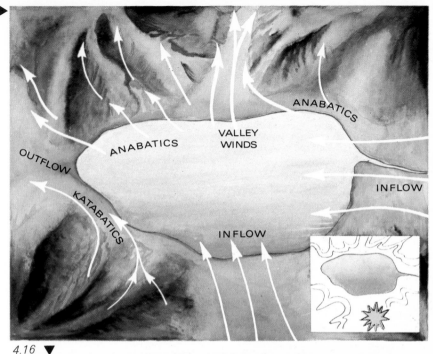

Local Topography

Return now to the map or chart of the area. Try to plot main features likely to influence the wind thermally. Note the paths which the wind will prefer. Wind is lazy and always goes the easy way. On small lakes, gaps in ranges of hills can provide the inlets or exits for wind either as a prevailing gradient flow or when feeding thermal influences. Remember that sunny slopes generate rising air, dark slopes mean falling air, and resulting winds can be very violent at times (4.15).

Lakes or ponds with low or flat shores scarcely influence the prevailing wind or, if near the coast, the seabreeze pattern. One should note obstructions to the wind, whether they are obvious such as buildings and trees or the less obvious slight undulations in the land surrounding the lake. The wind prefers to follow a low-lying course and so should be stronger where the shore is lowest. It will fan out from this area or converge into it depending on the direction of the prevailing flow (4.16).

4.16 ▼

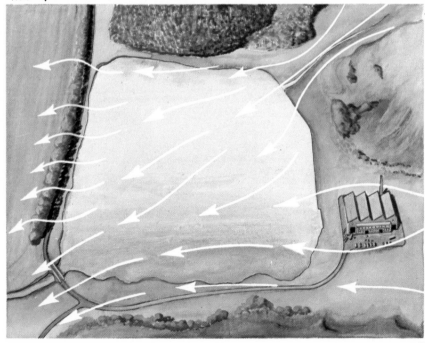

◀ 4.17

Solid obstructions such as buildings have considerable turbulence in lee and quite violent draughts through gaps (4.17). Trees on the other hand have a much softer effect on the wind and sometimes more wind gets through low down. Hence it can pay to go close to a weather shore which has trees than to sail farther out where there is more turbulence from the bushy upper branches.

Remember also that the wind has to rise to get over obstructions on the lee side of the course and there will be a dead area close to the obstruction (4.18).

Similarly on open coasts note where river valleys meet the sea. The wind will draw up these or fan out from them. It will rise well before it meets a cliff thus leaving a dead zone (4.19). If parallel to a coast expect stronger winds at headlands, lighter winds in bays often accompanied by marked shifts (4.20). There will be stronger winds parallel to a long high coast but beware of violent falling winds coming through gorges, cliffs or dark valleys. On a larger scale, a mountainous hinterland can generate strong falling winds over a wide area such as the mistral, bora or tramontana of the Mediterranean. Seabreeze effects often lessen their strength in the middle of the day but they can dominate the weather for several days at a time.

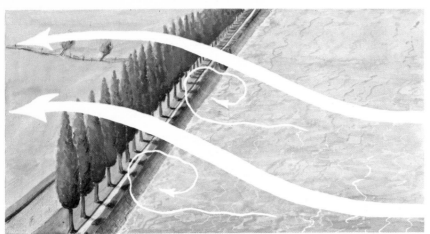

▲ 4.18

◀ 4.19

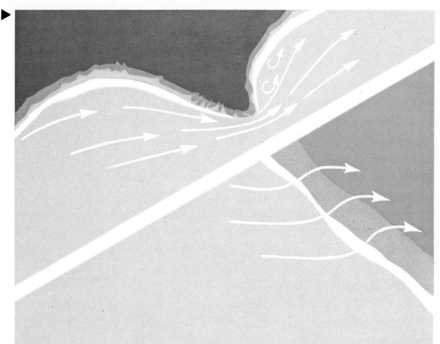

One more effect to note is wind-bend over a coast. The flow tends to cross the actual coast more at right angles and this fact has a tactical use as will be seen later (*4.21*).

Local current effects

Another influence on race strategy is the current. Even in areas where there is said to be no current there is often a wind-induced flow in the upper water layers which can be significant. On the sea or estuary the current can frequently win or lose a race and must therefore be studied.

Back to the chart then to see what can be learnt. Nautical charts and almanacs give tidal information often in the form of tidal chartlets with recorded speeds and directions every hour. The extremes at neap and spring tides are also given (*4.22*).

The sailing instructions should give the times of high tide. If not they can be got from tide tables, by asking the club or harbour-master, or even being heard on local radio or read in the newspaper. Certain charts give the strength and direction of tides, at both Springs and Neaps, at selected points, often known as tidal diamonds from their shape. From them work out the directions and strength for the area you are using and mark them nearby on the chart (*4.23*). Apart from plotting the most favourable course it is vital to know this when approaching a mark in the dark for example.

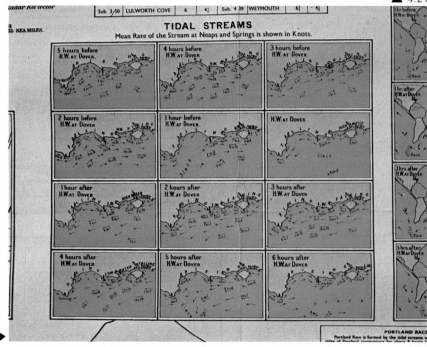

TIDAL STREAMS
Mean Rate of the Stream at Neaps and Springs is shown in Knots.

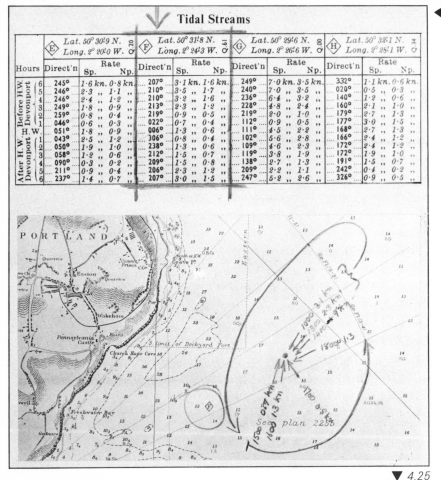

Tidal Streams

		Lat. 50° 30.9 N. Long. 2° 20.0 W. (E)			Lat. 50° 31.8 N. Long. 2° 24.3 W. (F)			Lat. 50° 29.6 N. Long. 2° 26.6 W. (G)			Lat. 50° 32.1 N. Long. 2° 28.1 W. (H)		
Hours		Direct'n	Rate Sp.	Np.	Direct'n	Rate Sp.	Np.	Direct'n	Rate Sp.	Np.	Direct'n	Rate Sp.	Np.
Before H.W. Devonport	6	245°	1·6 kn.	0·8 kn.	207°	3·1 kn.	1·6 kn.	249°	7·0 kn.	3·5 kn.	332°	1·1 kn.	0·6 kn.
	5	246°	2·3 ,,	1·1 ,,	210°	3·5 ,,	1·7 ,,	240°	7·0 ,,	3·5 ,,	020°	0·5 ,,	0·3 ,,
	4	246°	2·4 ,,	1·2 ,,	210°	3·2 ,,	1·6 ,,	236°	6·4 ,,	3·2 ,,	140°	1·2 ,,	0·6 ,,
	3	249°	1·8 ,,	0·9 ,,	213°	2·3 ,,	1·2 ,,	228°	4·8 ,,	2·4 ,,	160°	2·1 ,,	1·0 ,,
	2	259°	0·8 ,,	0·4 ,,	219°	0·9 ,,	0·5 ,,	219°	2·0 ,,	1·0 ,,	179°	2·7 ,,	1·3 ,,
	1	046°	0·6 ,,	0·3 ,,	022°	0·7 ,,	0·4 ,,	112°	0·9 ,,	0·5 ,,	177°	3·0 ,,	1·5 ,,
H.W.		051°	1·8 ,,	0·9 ,,	006°	1·3 ,,	0·6 ,,	111°	4·5 ,,	2·2 ,,	168°	2·7 ,,	1·3 ,,
After H.W. Devonport	1	043°	2·5 ,,	1·2 ,,	306°	0·8 ,,	0·4 ,,	102°	5·6 ,,	2·8 ,,	166°	2·4 ,,	1·2 ,,
	2	050°	1·9 ,,	1·0 ,,	238°	1·3 ,,	0·6 ,,	109°	4·6 ,,	2·3 ,,	172°	2·4 ,,	1·2 ,,
	3	058°	1·2 ,,	0·6 ,,	212°	1·5 ,,	0·7 ,,	119°	3·8 ,,	1·9 ,,	172°	1·9 ,,	1·0 ,,
	4	090°	0·3 ,,	0·2 ,,	209°	1·5 ,,	0·8 ,,	138°	2·7 ,,	1·3 ,,	191°	1·5 ,,	0·7 ,,
	5	211°	0·9 ,,	0·4 ,,	206°	2·3 ,,	1·2 ,,	209°	2·2 ,,	1·1 ,,	242°	0·4 ,,	0·2 ,,
	6	237°	1·4 ,,	0·7 ,,	207°	3·0 ,,	1·5 ,,	247°	5·2 ,,	2·6 ,,	326°	0·9 ,,	0·5 ,,

▼ 4.25

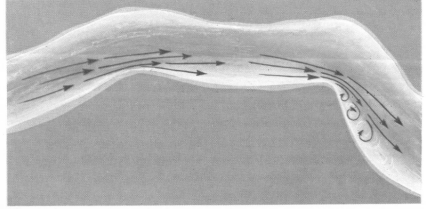

◀ 4.23 Typical tidal information with estimated speeds and directions marked in for the period of the race

For the offshore racer tidal information is a normal part of navigation and pilotage but for the small boat sailor racing on a tight course there is neither time nor facility for doing the work on board. You have to study the information ashore and transfer the significant points to a noteboard.

You must know the current speed and direction at the start (and up to an hour later in case of delay), the time it changes and the local sea bottom contours so that you can work out its tactical influence.

Even more than the wind, the current takes the easy path but it cannot rise up and over an obstruction which breaks surface. This means a sharp cut-off as the tide uncovers a shoal, for example, with a big change in the current direction and strength (4.24).

Basically the current is slower in shallow water and faster in deep channels but it is also faster near obstructions. It fans and converges in the same way as wind.

Currents swing out when following curving channels or rounding headlands so there is less current on the inside of the bend. If the corner is sharp, or the spit or headland is pronounced, there may be a reverse eddy on the down-current side of it (4.25). It is usually absolutely essential to take maximum advantage of such a feature.

Watch out also for sharp dividing lines between two currents, often marked by a line of scum on the surface or by floating debris or even by a change in the colour of the water. To be one side or the other of this line could make a vital difference to the result of the race.

Draw out the pattern of currents on the chart and it will immediately be seen how this can be used to plan the best course.

Sea and wave

There is one more piece of local knowledge that is needed before the final strategy of the race is decided. Sea and wave conditions can have a marked effect on boat speed.

Experience of your particular boat and its behaviour will tell you the sort of waves which are of a length and height that are awkward to sail through. The main difficulty is going to windward when waves of a particular length will cause the boat to slam or to hobby-horse.

The basic guides are as follows:

● *In tideless waters* the waves are shorter and lower where it is shallow; longer and higher where it is deep.

● *In fresh water* (which includes the Baltic) waves are steeper and the boat feels sluggish because it floats deeper in the less dense fluid. Boats do not plane so readily. Tactics must be modified accordingly.

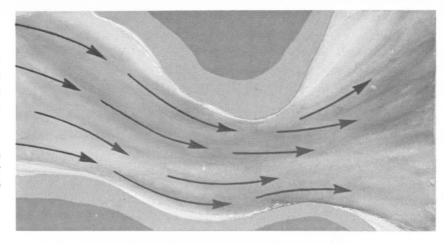

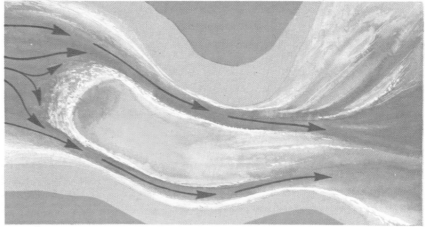

4.24 ▲   ▼ 4.26

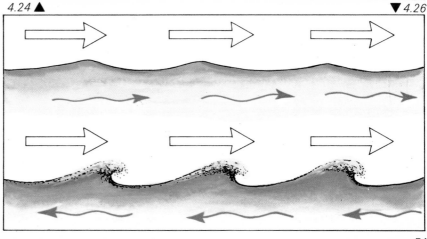

continued overleaf

◀ 4.27 The shoal water is on the right
and the current is moving to the left

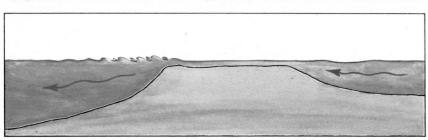

◀ 4.28

● *In currents* which are moving against the wind the sea is steeper and the waves more likely to break. Sea moving with the wind is longer, lower and more rounded (*4.26*). It is often possible in the middle of the English Channel, for example, to tell the state of the tide simply from looking at the waves.

● *In currents*, shoaling water or obstructions are marked by short, steep breaking waves which start immediately down-current of the shoal (*4.27*). Often the top of the shoal has particularly smooth water (*4.28*).

● *The stronger the wind* and the longer it has blown, the bigger are the waves. Depending on the depth of water these may break dangerously or be very difficult to sail through.

● *In continuing gales* with a long fetch (distance from the nearest windward land) waves may break heavily in depths as great as ten fathoms (20 metres).

Strategically your course planning should allow for known hazards, such as Portland Race in the English Channel, for example, well known to British and French offshore racers or Long Island Sound's race in the United States. The time of arrival should be estimated and action, either to sail through the race or make a detour, should start to be taken well in advance.

On small scale courses the current, and hence the waves, may be very different on parts of the course and will dictate the best route, perhaps within very narrow limits and thus seriously affect the inter-boat tactics that can be used.

Tactical use can also be made of waves and currents by leading or forcing opponents into unfavourable areas by means of the right-of-way rules.

Chapter 5

Tactics
and the Wind

5.1 ▲   ▼ 5.3

5.2 ▲   ▼ 5.4

5.5   A 'seabreeze window'

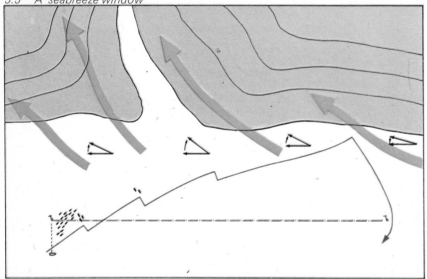

5.6 ▲

5.7   Cumulus building towards thunder

Using the forecasts

Before you go afloat you should now realise that you must *know* the types of weather situations you will be faced with.

For example: there is a depression approaching and you have discovered the expected time of arrival of the first warm front, which turns out to be in the middle of your race (5.1). Prepare for:

Lowering cloud and rain with increasing wind (5.2). The *mean* speed will be given in the forecast but expect it to be stronger at sea near coasts. Look for veering shifts (clockwise) as first the warm and then the cold fronts go through (5.3) though they may not be entirely clear cut (5.4—after a cold front).

Tactically, you obviously set up the boat and crew for fresh winds and rain, but the over-riding factor is to take advantage of the expected veering shift. If offshore racing, you should plot the expected new wind direction and work out what position you can reach by the time it arrives to be able to go for the mark fastest. Then set a course to get near that point. Or perhaps you realise that the shift when it comes will cause you to overstand the windward mark. Therefore in such a case you might start sailing with sheets eased well before it arrives.

On a small inshore course you have to keep a sharp lookout. You cannot predict exactly the time that the shift will arrive which may be when you are beating or running or even as you are rounding a mark. A close watch on the sky and the compass is the only safeguard and you should start each leg in expectation of an imminent veer.

Another more involved example: a light gradient wind and clear skies are forecast. It sounds like a good seabreeze day but the possibility of thunder inland is also forecast. From your study of the topography there is a good 'seabreeze window' inland opposite the course area (5.5) and you notice signs of cumulus starting to build. The wind is force 3 parallel to the coast and so you start on the offshore end of the line so that you are to windward of the opposition and you take the tack inshore first (5.6). The seabreeze effect will start to pull the gradient wind inshore and it will be strongest near the beach as well as lifting you on the inshore tack. Be prepared to

take short hitches offshore to remain just to weather of the other boats since you will all be continually lifted as the wind draws shorewards.

This is an example of how to balance two opposing features—increasing wind inshore favouring inshore boats; a freeing wind on the inshore tack favouring the windward boats.

Later on in the race you notice that the cumulus inland is starting to build into massive piles with dark bases (5.7). Thunderstorms will affect the seabreeze and, if extensive, can kill it completely. Not only that, there is a cold outflow from thunder clouds which can effectively reverse even the gradient wind.

Expect the wind to revert to its original direction with the possibility of sudden gusts directly off shore. Perhaps you should in general keep inshore and expect a

difficult and anxious time watching for smoke and other clues and trying to cover the rest of the fleet.

Clouds and gusting winds
There are some general rules about clouds and weather which are of tactical use:

● Small clouds mean smaller wind-shifts and less violent gusts.
● Large clouds mean large wind-shifts and heavy squalls.
● Sheet cloud at low level or complete overcast means stable airstreams and little gusting or local shifting.

Cumulus shows where there are columns of rising air. The loss of air at the surface has to be replaced and so air falls again between the clouds, more strongly close to the leading edge of the clouds as they advance (5.8). Under a well broken sky with scattered cumulus the wind will gust under the leading edge of clouds and will be felt as a veering shift (N. Hemisphere).

▼ 5.8

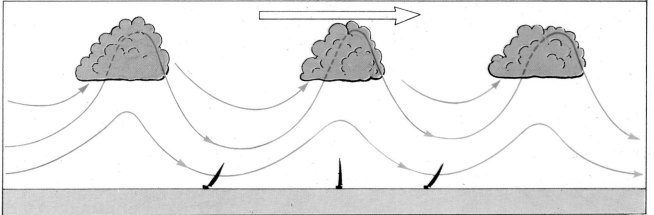

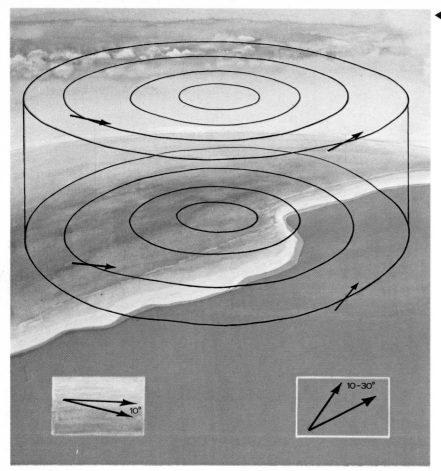

The veer with the gust is greater over land areas than it is over the sea owing to the greater effect of surface friction on the air-flow. The upper air blows nearly parallel to the isobars. At the surface however the friction effect angles the wind more towards the Low or away from the High centres (5.9). The angle is of the order of 10° over the sea and 30° over land in temperate latitudes. Round a Low it backs in the Northern Hemisphere and veers in the Southern Hemisphere. This fact immediately opens up tactical possibilities when sailing near coasts across which the gradient wind is blowing since there has to be a windshift of up to 20° somewhere over the coastal zone. Coupled with the steering effect of wind going up estuaries or passing through gaps of lower land, the total windshift could be very marked on some parts of the course (5.10).

Analysis of a gusting airstream

If we could take a sideways look at a section of wind it could be seen that it has a more or less turbulent flow. The surface friction effect causes tumbling in the lower layers. If there are thermal effects as well such as when a cold air-stream is continually dropping and being warmed in contact with a warmer sea, then the air layers could be very turbulent. This tumbling is often but not always, marked by cumulus cloud as heaps of warmed air rise only to be cooled again and become available for further falling (5.11).

As the air rises and cools it joins the upper air and picks up its speed and direction. When it falls it still has the upper air speed and direction thus reaching the surface as a veering gust (Northern Hemisphere).

It hits the surface and rapidly dissipates its energy by fanning out and mixing with the slower surface air. As it fans and slows long fingers can tumble onwards for some distance and hence the picture to a surface observer is like a splayed hand which is pushing forward in the direction of the fingers (5.12). As the gust dies out it can be visualised as if the hand was closing when the fingers fold up as the hand moves forward. The 'clenched fist' of the gust gradually slows and dissipates as the hand turns to become parallel to the surface wind.

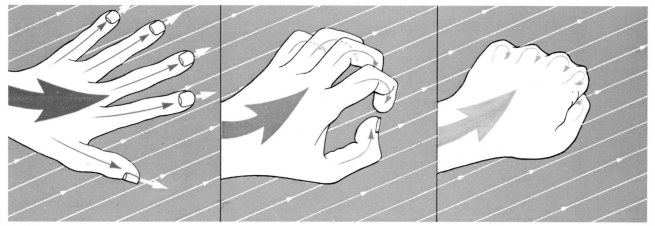

LIFT

SMALL LIFT

HEADING SHIFT

SMALL HEADER

NORMAL COURSE

Tactically, the helmsman must watch to windward. First, he must look for clouds which will be in his path or which can be put into his path by tacking beforehand. Second, he must work out which side of the leading edge of the cloud (and hence, the gust) his boat will be (5.13).

If there are no clouds or if the gusting is of the type where frequent small squalls come down the wind every half minute or so, advance planning is impossible. Each has to be dealt with as it appears as a dark flurry on the water to windward (5.16).

The questions to be answered are:
a) Will the gust reach me or will it disperse?
b) On which side of the gust will I be?

Then, with the plan of a standard gust pattern in your mind, work out if you should sail through it or tack and, if the latter, when to tack.

Some general rules can be given for dealing with typical gusts taken in isolation (reverse the advice for the Southern Hemisphere).

1 On starboard tack a boat will, in general, be freed or lifted by a gust, more so on the left side and less so on the right (5.14–A). In fact on the right side owing to the fanning effect, the wind may

5.14 ▼

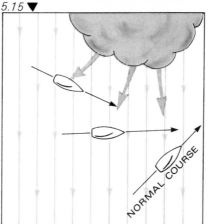

A

B

NORMAL COURSE

5.15 ▼

NORMAL COURSE

stay the same or even back a little (*B*), especially towards the rear of the gust.

2 On port tack the opposite occurs (*5.15*).

3 Ahead of a gust there is often a 'false gust'. The effect is a sudden sharp increase in windspeed followed immediately by a lull and then the main gust. During the false gust, the wind may *back* momentarily. You will not be deceived however if you watch the water where the main gust will still be obvious as a dark patch to windward, easily visible even in quite rough seas (*5.16*).

4 Behind the gust there is an area of generally less wind. In light winds this is a 'hole' which must be avoided and in these conditions it can cover a large area (*5.17*).

Tactically therefore, if a boat is on its own:

● On *port tack* a boat should tack if on the left or centre of the gust.

● On *starboard tack* it should tack if on the right side or if it will sail into the hole in the rear.

If other boats are involved, the knowledge of what will happen in a gust can enable a boat to break from cover or can give an opportunity for many yards to be gained by correct anticipation of the changes needed in boat handling.

5.17 ▶

5.18 A thunderstorm showing air being drawn towards the storm centre from all points and the violent outflow with rain around the leading edge

The gust-effect is seen to extreme either in light winds under cumulus cloud or in thunderstorm conditions. In both cases the variations in wind-speed and direction will be very much greater and will take longer to pass.

In light conditions boats can often be seen on the windward leg sailing close-hauled on courses 30° different. When thunder clouds are about, the cold outflow can be very violent and completely reverse the previous wind.

A big thunderstorm, marked by towering cumulus with a heavy black base, is drawing in air from all around to feed its central updraught. This can completely kill any prevailing wind, especially a seabreeze. One often only notices a slight breeze *towards* the storm which is utterly swept away by the down-draught as the cloud approaches. This is frequently accompanied by heavy rain which cascades from its leading edge (*5.18*).

An extensive thundery area can smother prevailing winds for hundreds of miles and, on the fringes, the weather is characterised by sudden increases in wind for a few minutes or half an hour, often shifting or even reversing the previous wind.

This is the 'opportunist's' weather. Keep a sharp look-out and many places could be won.

Rhythmic wind-shifts

Rhythmic shifting occurs on any apparently steady wind and is frequently only accurately detectable on the compass. It is surprising how even such close observers as members of the race committee fail to notice quite marked windshifts and often give entirely the wrong reason to changes in the order of boats. It is easy also for inexperienced sailors to misinterpret a small shift as being a mysterious alteration in boat-speed or pointing angle (5.28). In general, steady winds do not occur, however much they may be sought after, with one or two possible exceptions, an example being for short mid-day periods off parts of the Californian coast or places where there is a strong draw through a gap between islands.

Rhythmic shifting can vary in period from a minute or so to perhaps twenty minutes (5.19). If shifts are at longer intervals or are erratic they may be caused by the passage of clouds or perhaps are due to seabreeze effects.

Shifts can be anything from a degree or two either side of a mean to at least ten degrees. If the shifts are much more than this, even up to 180°, they will be due to more obvious influences such as thunder or seabreeze.

Rhythmic shifting can be present under clear or cloudy skies but is unlike the shifting caused by unstable gusty air streams marked by cumulus or thundery clouds (5.20).

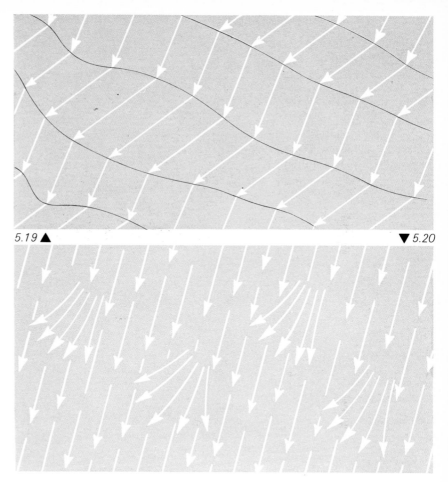

5.19 ▲   ▼ 5.20

From the tactical viewpoint the first thing to do is establish if it is there. This is done by getting on to the course early and sailing to windward, watching the compass and noting the times of any shifts of more than 4° or 5°. Keep near the starting area, so after ten minutes turn and run dead down-wind still noting the shifts on the compass and also the timing. If there is a pattern it will soon show up. Establish whether clouds are influencing the wind and also assess the pos-

sible effects of seabreeze.

Having established the wind-shift pattern, you only need to make check measurements until close to the starting time to be able to work out the likely time of the vitally important shift which will occur at or shortly after the start itself. Many a race has been won by getting this initial planning right. As a consequence a boat starting at apparently the wrong end of the line on the wrong tack can make it

5.21 Using a tactical compass.
Many compasses have a moveable grid ring like this one. The parallel lines are the grid and revolve complete with the cover glass. The red, green and orange lines have been stuck onto this glass too and so revolve with it.

Set the grid pointer to the true or the mean wind direction (336° in this case). The green and red lines show the approximate headings on starboard and port tack. If the compass needle moves into the angle between these lines you are sailing on a lift or a freeing shift. In the picture the pointer indicates we are sailing on a small heading shift on starboard tack. Remember that the

pointer is North and is not the ship's heading. It is easier to think of the grid lines as being the bow relative to the pointer when sailing to windward.

The orange lines are the theoretical start line. Aim the boat along the line. If the pointer is above the line the port (red arrow) or starboard (green arrow) end pays by the number of degrees it is away from the orange line.

You can also mark references on the grid for reaching and running if you like. You should note the compass courses between marks onto the deck panel or note-board. See also Chapter 7 for more information.

all come right a few minutes later when the expected shift arrives, and the clever crew is then well to windward (x) of the fleet (Boat A in *5.22*) and especially so of boats starting at the opposite end (B). Of course everyone says afterwards that they were so lucky but, to be

perfectly honest, there is very little luck amongst the winners at yacht racing. There is not much that cannot be foreseen with a careful and intelligent eye and it is good mental training to tell this fact to oneself constantly especially when things go wrong.

The crew should keep track of rhythmic shifting during the whole race. Things to watch for are:

1 Approaching the weather mark, will it be preferable, on account of the wind direction at that moment, to come into the mark on port tack (i.e. without right-of-way)? Is there room to do this?
2 Will a shift one way or the other cause the spinnaker to be set on a different side?
3 Approaching the lee mark, which is going to be the favourable tack at the beginning of the next windward leg?
4 Finally, when approaching a windward finishing line, is there likely to be a shift at the last minute and, if so, how can I ensure that the nearest boats are covered?

The main use of rhythmic windshifts concerns getting the boat around the course fastest. In other words—sailing the shortest distance. A simple diagram can show that on a windward leg a freeing shift gets you nearer to the windward mark (*5.23–A*). Conversely, a header takes you away from the mark (B). This leads to one of the best known basic tactical rules:

● Stay with a freer (or lift)
● Tack on a header (or knock)

A header on one tack of course becomes a freer on the other hence, if this rule is followed in a shifting wind, it should mean that the shortest track is taken (*5.24*). The diagram shows the theoretically

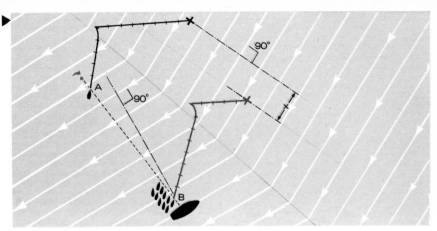

best (Black) and worst (Red) courses. Unfortunately like almost all rules in yacht racing, it does have its exceptions though most are obvious when thought about:

1 Before tacking try to make sure that a header really is going to stay for an appreciable period by watching the water to windward.

2 Similarly, make sure it is not going to continue to head in stages and so do not tack too early.

3 Some headers are so local, for example, a small gust, that the boat sails out of it again almost as soon as it has tacked.

4 Make sure that the type of boat you are using is capable of benefiting from tacking; i.e. if it is a genuine long-term shift of only 3° it would pay for any boat even a large ocean racer, to tack. Only the most manoeuvrable of small boats should tack on small brief headers.

5 Watch the course. A tack which would put you beyond the layline to the windward mark after the next freeing shift would normally be a losing tactic.

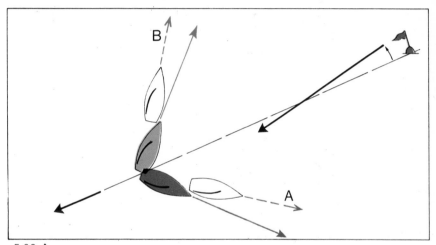

5.23 ▲

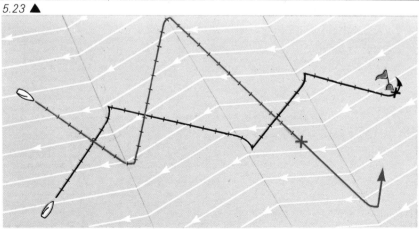

5.24 ▶

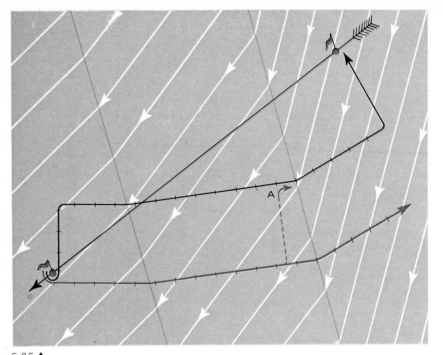

Exceptions to the rules

The rule to stay with a freer or lift also has its exceptions. It works if the lift is part of a rhythmic pattern though, if you experience such a lift, it means that you had previously got the pattern wrong. You ought to have been on the other tack.

The most frustrating type of shift is a lift which continues to free by stages (*5.25*). If you are expecting it and have taken steps to be to windward of the opposition then you can only benefit (black). But all other boats must lose and those on the opposite side of the course can drop from first to nearly last in a few short minutes (red).

The only answer for a boat so caught is to cut its losses and tack over towards the freeing side (*A*). Unless you think it is going to lift still more, it will be best to tack back just to leeward of the windward boats but it can only be a salvage operation which, at best, can enable you to keep in touch with the leaders in the hope of another chance of recovering later on.

There is one type of lift which gives the lead to the leeward boats. This is when it is so great that the windward leg becomes a reach even for those furthest to leeward (*5.26*). However, a lift of this magnitude should have been foreseen in the weather planning or on account of clouds and thunder being present.

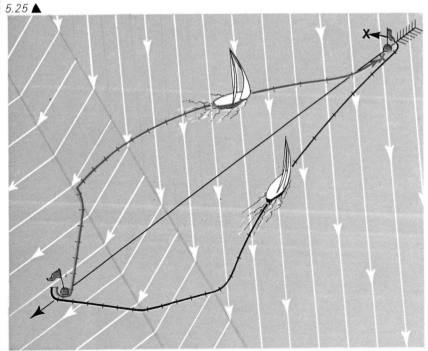

Always keep in mind that wind-shifts do not usually arrive on the course perpendicular to the existing wind. They reach the left or the right side first. If the expected shift is towards the left then almost always the shift will reach the left side of the course first. This leads to the next basic tactical rule:

● Sail towards the expected shift.

But not too far (see para 5, page 63). In the case of a major change such as the replacement of a dying seabreeze with a prevailing wind from the opposite direction, the exact positioning of the boat is critical and the timing is crucial (5.27). The problem is not only which side of the course (the leader (red) loses) but how far to sail to meet the shift. Not far enough and someone else will pick it up first and sail right around you; too far (blue) and boats to leeward (black) who feel it later will still have the shortest distance to go. It is easy in such circumstances to become completely disorientated. If there is time, have a look at the chart. The changes in angles and courses will then be immediately obvious and the right decision is easier to make.

Slow wind-shifts are the most difficult to detect but, for this reason alone, are among the most valuable of tactical weapons. So few crews realise they are there and later wonder why the winner (black) was so lucky (5.28).

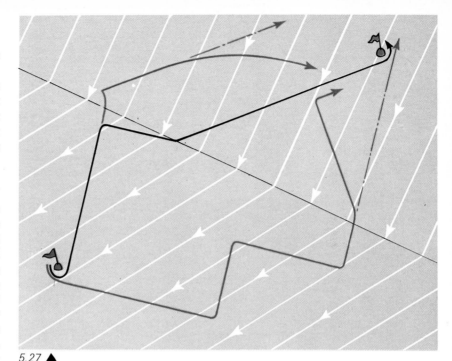

5.27 ▲

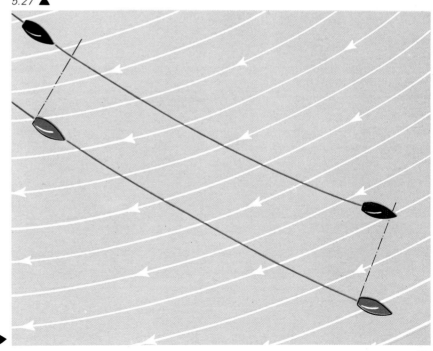

5.28 ▶

There are three main causes of slow wind-shifting:

1 Gradual re-alignment of isobars around a moving weather system. This is particularly typical ahead of an approaching Low.
2 Seabreeze or other local thermal influence on an existing wind (4.12).
3 Rotational shifting caused by the earth's rotation underneath an established wind.

The first case should have been spotted and taken into account in the pre-race planning because it it stems from information given in the forecast.

The passage of fronts which give

5.29 ▼

more or less sudden and definite shifts was discussed earlier but not the slow shifting resulting from the change in position or development of a weather system. The drawing (5.29) shows the expected shifts relative to a fixed point above, in line with, and below an advancing Low. Highs do not usually move much and so do not produce tactically useful shifts of this type.

The normal rule—sail towards the expected shift—applies but, when the shift is slow and relatively steady, the tactic is not to sail to extremes. It is only necessary to keep just nearer the expected shift than the chief opposition.

Therefore, on a windward leg you concentrate on the side of the

course nearest to the expected shift and you tack to cover any boats which show a tendency to move that way, always trying to keep just outside them until you reach the lay line.

Here is an ideal opportunity to use 'herding' tactics to keep the most dangerous opponents under control; this tactic will be explained in detail later (9.14 et seq).

The second case involves your own observations of the likelihood of local thermal winds. The development of such wind will influence the prevailing air-flow and cause a shift in its direction as the thermal effect builds up. Conversely the shift will reverse as the thermal effects die down.

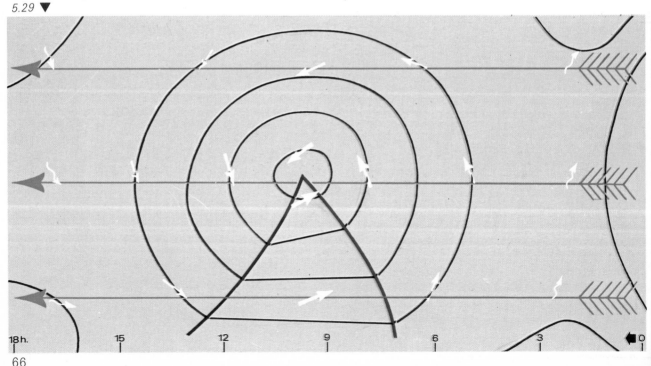

18h.   15   12   9   6   3   0

It is necessary to know from the forecast what the prevailing wind force and direction will be. Then the thermal effect, caused by sun or lack of sun on coastal land or mountain slope, can be plotted together with its likely duration.

For example, seabreeze in a certain area may start to affect the prevailing wind from, say, 11.00 increasing to a maximum around 15.30 and dying away at 18.00.

A prevailing wind will be modified in direction, and also can vary in strength, as witness the reduction in force with the day of an offshore mistral, itself a thermally induced wind.

The tactics on the race course

5.30 ▼

are basically the same—work over towards the expected shift—but in this case remembering to change to the other side as the thermal influence dies.

The third cause of slow windshifts—the rotational effect—is perhaps the least understood. Inevitably one's own store of significant instances is coloured either by dramatic success or disastrous failure. I can remember this particular effect being forever impressed on my mind by two unexpected wins in a world championship series many years ago, the second resulting from profiting from the first, and since then it has become one of the many semiautomatic mental checks that I make when racing and are

5.31 ▼

examples of things which come with experience.

Imagine that you are looking down on the North Pole from a great height (*5.30*). There is a wind blowing across it which you can gauge from the clouds and driven snow. An hour later its direction relative to the surface has veered (clockwise) by exactly 15° (360° in 24 hours). The reason is that the wind is a solid moving airmass relatively unconnected to the earth's surface and the earth is revolving underneath it.

This fact explains why, for example, the wind does not blow directly from, say, the Azores High to the Polar Lows but instead angles more and more westerly the

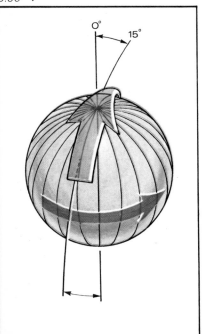

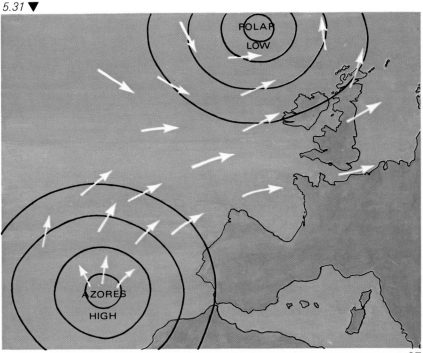

further North it goes, the effect being nil at the equator increasing to a maximum at the Pole (5.31). It explains the prevailing South-West winds of North-Western and central Europe. It explains why the wind follows the isobars (modified somewhat by surface frictional effects) counter-clockwise round a Low (Northern Hemisphere) and clockwise round a High.

These facts are all useful when working out what the wind and weather will do but the earth's rotation has one other significant and particularly local effect which is of tactical value to racing sailors. What we have mentioned above are the long-term effects on weather on a large scale which result in more or less permanent changes in prevailing wind. But the same effect is noticed on a local wind which only lasts a short time.

Thus a seabreeze, although only lasting a few hours, consists of a moving mass of many thousands or millions of tons of air. Once underway its direction is not easily changed because even though it cannot be seen it has enormous mass and so it too will appear to veer with time.

Hence the often quoted rule that the wind appears to shift with the sun. This means that it shifts with the progress of the day and, when it does it tends to veer (in the Northern Hemisphere). It is most marked on East, South and West facing coasts and is a reason why,

68

under such conditions, you should work the starboard side of the windward leg.

So the rule is (for the Northern Hemisphere):

● A local wind will tend to veer with time.

Points to watch are:
1 A local wind is more likely to veer over an unobstructed area such as an open sea coast with a flat hinterland than a wind which is 'steered' by river valleys or estuaries or by gaps in hills or mountain chains.
2 The veer is seldom slow and even. It shifts in an erratic series of jerks, sometimes shifting back a short way before veering again.
3 The commonest condition for this effect to be of tactical use is when there is sun and a sea-breeze blowing onshore.

Light airs
Light weather racing can be the most interesting tactically. All the features we have been discussing tend to be more exaggerated in light weather and the thermal influences are proportionally greater. Many sailors believe that wins in light airs are mostly due to luck but a study of individual results shows that this cannot be so. The same helmsmen win too often.

For successful light air sailing you need patience, absolute concentration and vigilance. Not only that, always keep in mind the fact

that in light airs the possible gains are many times greater than in medium or heavy winds. This is simply because every boat has a maximum hull speed which is hard to exceed without planing. This speed is easily reached in medium winds, after which improvements are comparatively less profitable. In light airs boat-speed is all important since there is the possibility of increasing it from zero to near the maximum hull speed with only a small actual increase in wind speed (5.32).

The search for the best wind and the tactics to exploit it are the helmsman's first aims and it is sometimes worth going far out of the direct line to get a better wind or a more favourable current or to avoid some obstruction to the airflow.

It is likely to be disastrous to be caught in a calm patch only to watch the others sail by outside it. Therefore the points to watch are:

1 Remember that gusts have 'holes' immediately behind (to windward) of them. Avoid tacking on a header straight into one (5.17).
2 Sail towards advancing clouds where a down-draught wind should be found under the leading edge (5.13 to 5.18).
3 Watch for thermal effects by keeping an eye on smoke, other sails, dark patches of ripples near the horizon and also clouds.
4 Remember that, when seabreeze is present, there will be a calm zone parallel to the shore which

moves offshore as the breeze strengthens and returns as it weakens. The cut-off can be very sudden from, say, Force 3 to zero (4.9).

5 In light winds the cut-up wind from the sails of other yachts or from obstructions extends a long way and it takes a long time to re-establish smooth air-flow. Avoid getting into such areas.

6 When starting in a large fleet there can be a significant lift on port tack (5.33). Useful when trying to recover from a poor start.

7 Finally, in light airs, 'weather tactics' and the effort to keep up boat-speed are usually far more important and profitable than inter-boat tactics. However, once a lead has been established the main concentration must be on covering the chief opposition. Do not try to cover too closely but keep in the general area while at the same time searching for the best wind.

An example of a seabreeze calm zone occurred on June 16th 1974 during a race for One-Tonners where the wind had been light off-shore at the start around 11.00 and nearly an hour later the situation was as in the diagram (5.34).

It was an unusual day in that it looked to be perfect for seabreeze but the prevailing wind, though light, was reinforcing the off-shore night breeze and was tending to increase. It was misty and thus the cumulus inland which heralded the start of the seabreeze was slow to

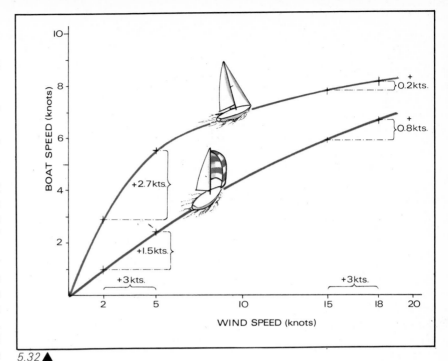

5.32 ▲

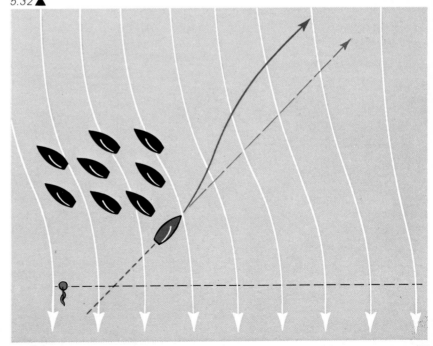

5.33 ▲

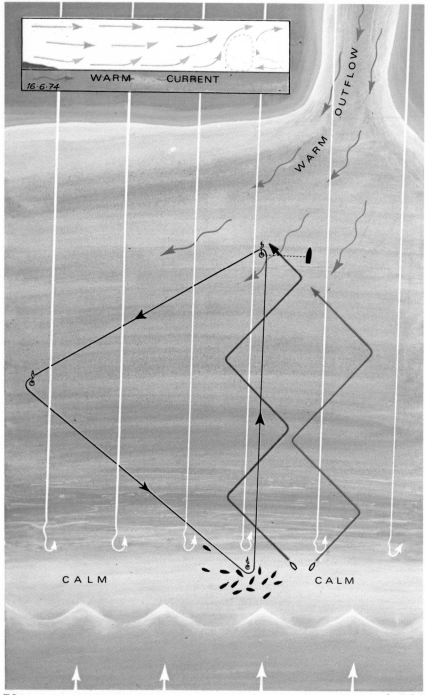

WARM OUTFLOW

WARM CURRENT

16·6·74

CALM

CALM

begin building. The result was a fight but the calm zone of the sea-breeze front, which is normally over the beach and which then moves inland, had been pushed out by the prevailing wind aided also by the tide which had started ebbing from the inland creeks of Chichester Harbour at about 07.30 bringing with it water which was substantially warmer than the sea. The front stuck about two miles offshore by the lee mark.

Seventy-five yards offshore of the mark the wind was an on-shore seabreeze. Fifty yards in-shore of the mark it was the off-shore prevailing wind. All the boats piled into this calm strip, as their spinnakers collapsed, and waited in a bunch to see who would win the fight, the off-shore prevailing wind or the on-shore seabreeze.

For some minutes nothing appeared to happen except that the two leading boats gradually approached the shoreward side of the calm on a very slight current. They started to feel the breeze, sheeted in their sails and were soon a mile away to windward while the rest of us watched and waited.

No one else reached the off-shore breeze because the seabreeze gradually gained mastery, the calm zone slowly worked shorewards and we went with it under spinnakers as the fitful leading puffs of the seabreeze pushed us before it. For the rest of the day there was a Force 3 on-shore seabreeze whose

▲ 5.34

outer calm zone, where the descending air reached the surface to feed it, was several miles offshore. We started a night race as this breeze was starting to die, finally all kedging five miles off-shore in the outer calm zone of the failing seabreeze (5.35).

Forty-five minutes later the land had cooled enough for the offshore night wind, reinforced by an increasing prevailing wind, to return sweeping the calm away and eventually reaching Force 5 during the early hours of the morning.

This fairly typical example could have been confusing to a boat's crew on account of the calm zone which was in this case the one which should have been over the inland area. However, it was immediately obvious that this was the case because the wind was blowing *towards* the calm zone before rising upwards whereas the normal outer calm zone, which is the one that is usually met at sea, has wind descending and blowing *outwards* from it (3.13).

Heavy weather
This is the opposite to light airs in more ways than just that (5.36). For example, close covering is not only most effective in these conditions but it is also very desirable to stick closely to the opposition. Boats are travelling at maximum hull-speed and the wind is fairly steady. There is usually little danger of falling into a 'hole' or of an unexpected wind-shift. There will only be small differences in boat-

5.35 ▲

5.36 ▲

speed to windward among a group of well-tuned boats, though, in dinghies, planing will be likely with the wind free.

Racing in heavy winds becomes much more a matter of boat handling techniques which can make big differences to results. Close-quarters tactics will be far more important than those relating to the weather. The tactics are to cover closely if ahead; to try to break clear if astern. Methods of doing

these are discussed in Part Three.

Boat-speed polar diagrams

Before we discuss boat-to-boat tactics, the relationship between wind angle, wind speed and boat-speed should be looked at so that helmsmen can have a mental picture of the effects of altering course a few degrees. It is not intended to analyse the subject in detail but simply to consider two different types of commonly used boat in two different wind speeds.

In the polar diagrams (5.37) the red lines represent the boat speeds at any heading angle to the TRUE wind of a fast planing dinghy, such as a 5–0–5, Flying Dutchman or similar, using trapeze and spinnaker. The blue lines represent a small racing keelboat using working sails and spinnaker only. The outer lines are typical for a moderate and steady planing breeze. The inner lines for a steady light breeze.

Note the extreme hump (high speed) caused by the power of the trapeze and the big sail area-to-weight ratio with the spinnaker (outer red line). Even in light winds the dinghy's spinnaker gives a great boost to speed though only over a fairly narrow range of wind angles (inner red line).

This small keelboat in contrast has a very low capacity for increasing its speed. In fresh winds it remains within a small margin of 6 knots for a very wide range of angles.

Note also the marked falling off in speed as the boats near a dead run—more so with the planing dinghy, as might be expected when it drops off the plane, and more for both types in the lighter wind, as is shown by the double humps at the bottom.

More interesting is how the

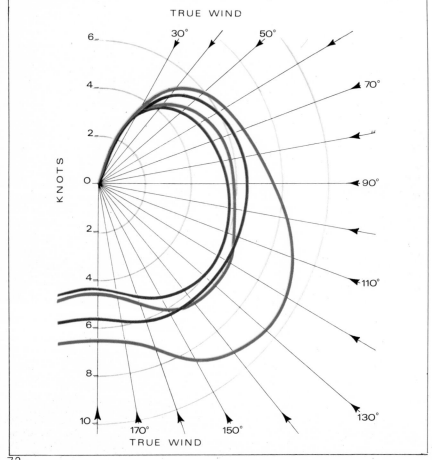

TRUE WIND

KNOTS

TRUE WIND

◀ 5.37

diagrams can show how much to aim off the direct line when tacking down wind (5.38). The keelboat hardly needs to aim off at all in the stronger winds. The dinghy on the other hand has a great capacity, especially in light winds, for increasing its speed dramatically by tacking downwind. Even more dramatic in this respect are catamarans which must always aim off downwind.

When thinking about these polar diagrams remember that the apparent wind is forward of the true wind and the amount depends on the boats' speed. For example the dinghy in the fresher wind might set a spinnaker with the apparent wind at about 95° to 100° to the boat's heading. This could be 130° to 140° to the true wind direction.

The problems of getting accurate readings and hence accurate curves are too great to be a practicable possibility for racing crews. The differences in optimum headings to windward and leeway angles are too small to be measured accurately and so the best pointing angle is usually found by trial and error and by experience (5.39). These diagrams are based on test sources and are put here to give food for thought and to encourage helmsmen to think about the invisible wind and how it acts on the sails.

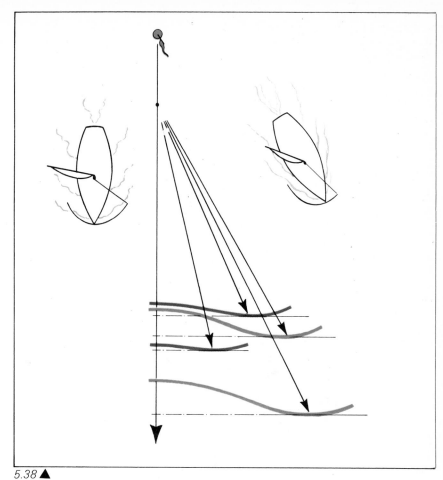

5.38 ▲

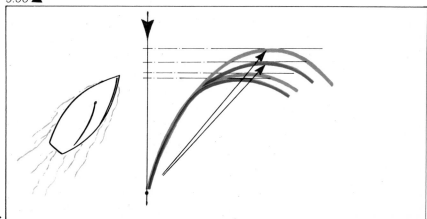

5.39 ▶

Chapter 6

Tactics and the Race Committee

Sum up your Committee

It may seem strange to have a chapter with such a heading but the attitude and actions of the Race Committee have a profound effect on the race. If you have never done duty with the flags, guns and watches then you should do so because until you understand the Race Committee's problems you will never know what to look for when planning your race strategy (*6.1*).

A few examples: Is your race being handled by a firm committee or one which is a little unsure of itself? If the first, you can be sure that the races will start on time, lines will be well laid, the rules will

6.1   The Race Committee

be strictly adhered to and boats over the line at the start will be noted and called back.

A weak committee will lay a poor line and then wonder why the boats are all bunching at one end. There will be many boats over at the start and there will be continual frustrating *General Recalls* and attempts to re-start without correcting the basic causes. There will be ambiguities in the sailing instructions, the course will be inaccurately laid, the race will be shortened at the slightest sign of wind failure or will not be started above Force 4 owing to shortage of patrol boats.

With the strong committee you know exactly where you are. You can plan your tactics sure in the knowledge that the race will be run like clockwork. The committee will make the most of the wind and current conditions and if they postpone, shorten or abandon the race, there will be sound reasons for doing so.

The weak committee's lack of experience or knowledge can sometimes be influenced by the voiced opinions of the sailors on the spot and, though a poorly laid line can be corrected in this way, it is a bad omen for the standard of the racing.

The practice race of a series should be a great opportunity for the committee, not only to test out all their arrangements, but to impress on the competitors that they

are going to be firm.

In a certain Finn Gold Cup series the committee fired recall guns at the start of the practice race but then did nothing more. They shortened the course unnecessarily and then posted a finishing order which did not penalize those which were over the line early. A practice race should be treated as a proper race, though separate from the championship itself, even having a small prize for the winner. Normal protest meetings should be held and the culprits disqualified. Instead, in this case the sailors instinctively got the message that this was a weak committee. The racing for the rest of the series was of a poor standard, there were a record number of general recalls and on one day racing had to be abandoned altogether after nine attempts to start. Hardly anyone was disqualified for being over the line early on the familiar grounds that there were others also whose sail

numbers could not be seen. In trying to be fair and kind they actually did everyone a disservice, so much so that even after very many years it sticks out in my mind as being one of the worst run championships that I have sailed in.

On another occasion a committee got what it deserved when it set a running start against a strong current on a line that was not only heavily biased towards the committee boat end but which had no inner distance mark and was also heavily favoured at that end on account of the current. Boats approaching the line to start reached a point where they blanketed those ahead and ran up on them and then found themselves unable to turn to the right or left on account of other boats. In the inevitable log-jam the committee boat was badly mauled by the fleet (*6.2*).

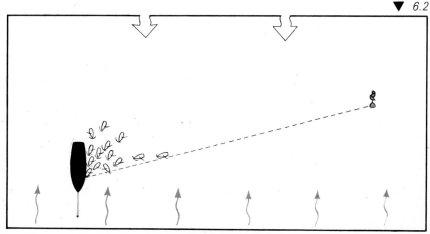

▼ *6.2*

75

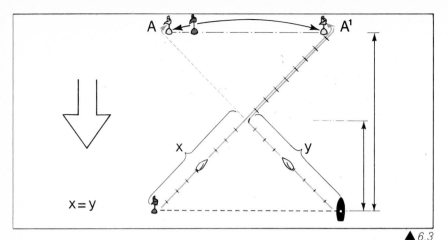

▲ 6.3

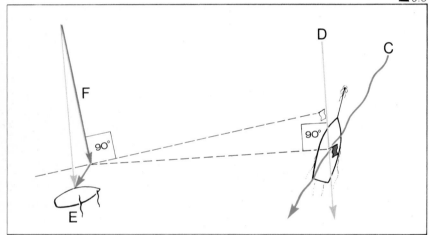

▲ 6.4

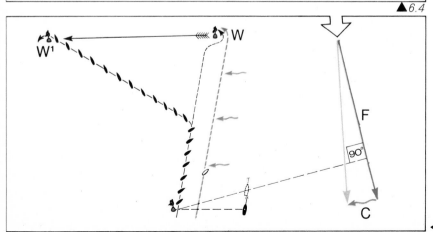

◄ 6.5

Course setting

Racing helmsmen should understand how a course is set because, not only are they then aware of the problems, but they can take tactical advantage of any errors which are made by the committee. So many sailors get very upset if the start line or the course is not perfect. It is *never* perfect and so the wise man will work out how to profit from the inevitable. Yacht racing is not a precise sport. Judgement is needed for almost every aspect of it.

All racing sailors know that a starting line for a windward leg has to be laid square to the wind and not square to the actual course so that any point within the close-hauled sector (*6.3*–A to A′) can be reached from either end of the line in the same time and the mark could be anywhere on this line. Few Race Committees realise however that the presence of a current (*6.4*–C) can mean that, though the line may be square to the wind for the anchored committee whose apparent wind direction is (D) it will look very different to the free-floating racing boats (E) whose apparent wind direction is shown by the vector (F) and the line ought to be laid perpendicular to this.

In (*6.5*) we have a situation with a current (C) coming from the side. The port end of the line is nearer to the apparent wind (F) and so not only is the line therefore wrongly laid but the weather mark (W) is also wrongly placed. To obtain a beat with an equal amount of sailing on port and starboard tacks it ought to have been at W'. This was the situation for more than half the races of a World Championship for Solings in which conditions were also so misty that mark finding was made particularly difficult.

When faced with such a course find out if, owing to the current, the windward mark can be fetched in one tack (green track) which is sometimes possible even from the more leeward end in light winds. If the wind eases all the boats will then find themselves reaching or even running to the mark against the current (dotted black track) and the leeward boats will have a substantial advantage both in boatspeed and distance.

Committees should measure the speed and direction of both wind and current and plot them to find the apparent wind which is being felt by the boats. A very easy way of checking the speed of the current is to use the 'Dutchman's Log' and to remember the useful formula:

● One yard or metre/sec nearly equals 2 knots.

The aim is to time the travel of a floating object over a set distance. Either throw a floating scrap overboard at the bow and time it when it passes a known mark further aft, or make a check-log with a piece of wood and fine line of a known length. Drop the float over the side

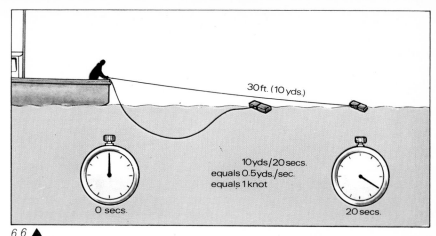

6.6 ▲

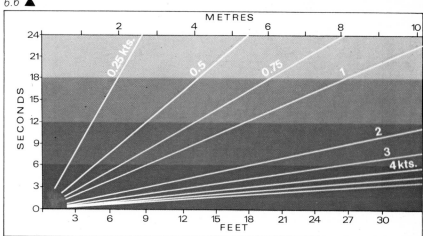

6.7 ▲

and time the period to when the line tightens (6.6). The graph gives the relationships between speed, time and distance (6.7).

Plot the true windspeed and direction (6.8–D) and the current speed and direction (C) as a vector triangle to get the apparent windspeed and direction for the boats (F). Set the weather mark in this direction and the start line square to it.

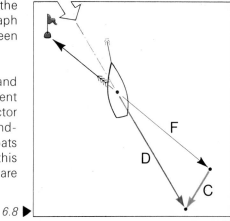

6.8 ▶

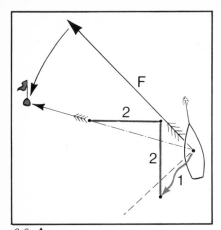

6.9 ▲

This still does not show the correct direction for the weather mark to give equal sailing on port and starboard tacks, which is a function of the boats' speed and the current speed.

The diagram (6.9) shows how to work it out assuming in this case that the boats are sailing at 4 knots (2 units plus 2 units) and the current is 1 knot (1 unit). If the weather mark has been placed to one side or the other of this ad-justed bearing you must be prepared to spend more time on one tack or the other and this knowledge might radically alter your starting tactics.

It is not feasible to make a complete analysis on board small boats though the race officer should certainly do so. However a quick check on the relative position of the windward mark can be made by sailing to windward on both tacks and noting its bearing. Remember that the mark should be *down current* of where it would be in still water.

Starting problems

The most important part of the race is the start. Once the boats have been got away on a fair line and are able to spread out, later variations in current or wind are more easily dealt with and can be allowed for by the committee in the positioning and order of rounding of the other marks.

Starting in currents is always difficult but many clubs all over the world have no option but to find the least unsatisfactory method. If the current is against at the start, the line should have been made longer since the boats will only just be able to cross it and will take up more room. The end nearest the shore, where the current will be less, will be favoured and so dropping this mark a little way down current helps prevent boats crowding the inshore end (6.10).

With a weather-going current

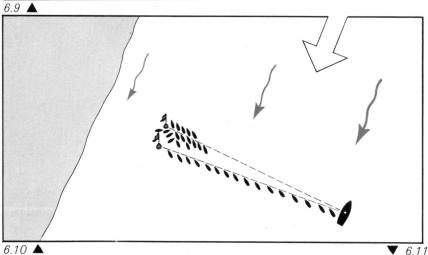

6.10 ▲   ▼ 6.11

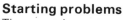

the committee boat should be moored fore and aft to hold her steady (*6.11*). Boats will almost certainly be over the line early and so a re-start is a near certainty unless a *one-minute rule* is included for the first start. If so it should have been clearly signalled and competitors warned in the Sailing Instructions and at the briefing meeting. The term 'one-minute rule' used here includes any other period that the Sailing Instructions may lay down and forbids boats from being across the line during the stated pre-start period (one minute in this case). The advantage is that it makes the fleet keep back from the line and, if any boats are over early, it gives the Race Officer a chance to get some sail numbers noted down in advance.

There are two possible consequences to being over the line during this period. In one, boats may re-start by *rounding the ends* of the line and getting acknowledgement from the committee (*6.12*). Much more severe, and to be used when a keen fleet is being particularly difficult, is to disqualify any boat which is over the line early with no option to return and re-start. On open water lines it is often best to have a one-minute rule for all starts and to delete the 'round-the-ends' facility if there has to be a 'General Recall' and a re-start.

Another reason for bad starts

6.12 ▲

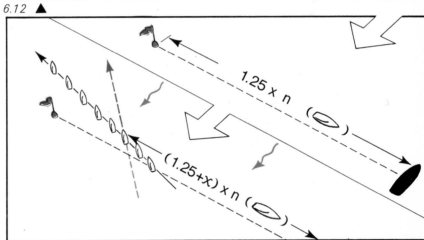

6.13 ▲

6.14 There is nearly always a sag in a long start line ▶

with many boats over prematurely is that the line is too short. The recommendation is one and a quarter times the total length of all the boats (6.13). More length is needed in light winds or a contrary current and less on reaching starts.

The effect of a line that is too short is for boats to press forward and to cause a bulge in the centre. On the contrary an over long line causes a sag in the centre (6.14).

Another point is that the length of line affects the amount of bias that is needed. Long lines are much more difficult to lay and should be more nearly square to the wind. Doubling the line length while retaining the same bias angle will double the advantage to a boat starting at that end. A perfect line would mean that boats starting from each end *on opposite tacks* would eventually collide. Since most boats start on starboard tack the boat at the port end is assumed to change tacks after starting and thus loses some distance (6.15– Red X to Black X). The line should be set so that thereafter they should be on collision courses (y=y). Hence the need for bias but it should really only amount to a boat's length for a racing dinghy and perhaps two or three lengths for an offshore racer.

Thus, recommended bias angles for open water and with no other influences could be as shown in the table (*right*).

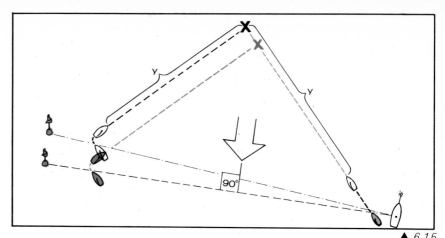

▲ 6.15

In cross currents the committee should first work out the apparent wind direction and speed for the boats and then apply the bias. There may also be other reasons for using more or less bias.

Running starts can be successful if they are made with the current but there are some points to watch. The angle of the line to the wind is not so important but the committee should ask themselves which end will be favoured on account of current or other influences and apply bias as nearly as possible to even out the differences.

The first mark after a running start should be starboard-handed if possible and the following leg should be to windward. Only in this way will all boats have a reasonable chance of sorting themselves out. If the mark is taken to starboard the race tends to begin again rather in the manner of a gate start, (6.29), and most boats get a reasonable start. Rounding to port means that leading boats can tack onto starboard and cause confusion at a very congested point. In either case, if the second leg is a reach the race will become a dull procession and so for the competitor, the position that he rounds this mark will decide the result of the race.

TABLE OF BIAS ANGLES

Length of Line (yds or m.)	100	200	300	500	800
Bias angle for Dinghies	6°	3°	2°	nil	nil
Keelboats	11°	6°	3°	2°	nil
40' Offshore Racers	—	11°	6°	$3\frac{1}{2}$°	2°

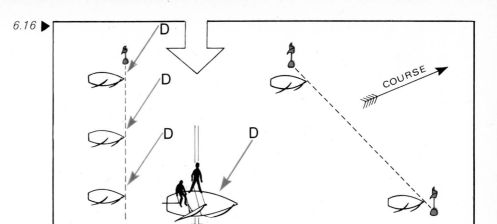

6.16 ▶

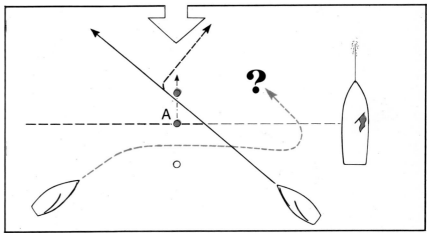

6.17 ▲

Reaching starts have little to commend them. If unavoidable it is best to arrange the first leg to be as nearly at right angles to the wind as possible and, starting from a standpoint that if the line cannot be square to the wind it should be at right angles to the course, to bias it carefully for the particular type of boat. For keel-boats there will be doubt amongst the competitors whether they can carry a reaching spinnaker. This may be enough to spread them fairly evenly along the line but usually a little bias in favour of the lee end will be best (6.16).

Trapeze dinghies will often be fastest close-reaching but if bias is given in favour of the windward end every boat except that to windward will be blanketed. Probably it will be best to set the line square to the course since the boats' speeds will bring their apparent wind well forward of the beam (D). The more nearly the first leg is a close reach the more bias should be given to the lee end until a line

which enables the weather mark just to be fetched should be square to the wind. The strategy for the sailor is to discover what the committee has done and to understand why. Then he can work out from his own position in his boat whether the committee has got it right or not. The best type of mistake is the small one because then you may be the only one to notice it!!

Laying marks

On windward starts the committee boat should be at the starboard end and normally would be protected by an inner distance mark (6.17–A) to keep boats away and give the line-judge a good view. This mark should be on the line or to windward of it. If it is to leeward there may be some doubt whether a boat can legally pass between it and the line before the start (6.20) and so it is wise to avoid this source of trouble (6.17).

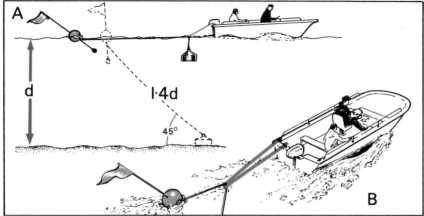

6.18 ▲

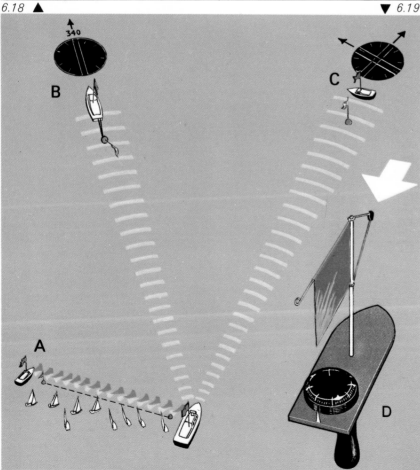

▼ 6.19

There should always be a small motorboat available in close contact with the committee ready to re-lay marks (6.18–A) (the anchor line should be 1½ times the depth of the water) or to drag either the outer or inner starting marks into new positions quickly (B). If sea conditions are difficult or if the wind is shifting or if the outer mark is an immovable buoy it may be best to abandon using an inner mark and to make sure that the committee boat itself can move easily and quickly. For this one needs plenty of anchor warp and two good anchors so that it can be moored bow and stern without dragging (6.11). Then the angle of the line can be adjusted by easing out one warp and hauling in on the other Committees should leave one more possibility open by having the line marked by a moveable post tied to the rail rather than the boat's fixed mast.

All these things should be known by a good race committee but not all committees are sufficiently experienced since most will be manned by amateur helpers Other things which are of signi ficance to the sailor are:

a) Is there a line-judge at both ends of the line (6.19–A)? If there is he should be in radio contact with the chief race officer and it will almost certainly mean that the committee will be tough at the start.

b) Are the marks being laid by radar? If so you can be sure that the positions will be particularly accurate. The other ways of laying the windward and gybe marks are to use a pelorus (D) and send boats off from the starting mark at known speeds and courses for known times (B) or to give the mark boats cross bearings on landmarks to find the required positions to drop the marks (C). Neither are as accurate as a radar fix and sometimes marks can be a long way out of position. Watch out also for marks which have dragged on the current. If a mark goes adrift, as happened for example in the final race of the 1974 One-Ton cup, the committee should replace it with a boat or another mark flying Flag M (white 'X' on a blue ground).

c) Will there be a path-finder launch to lead the way? This makes it very easy but do not neglect the pre-start checks because the path-finder will only be there for the first leg or possibly for the first round.

d) Are the limit marks exactly on the line or to windward or to leeward and if so by how much? A wise committee will place the mark as nearly on the line as possible. If it is some way to windward the boats tend to move up to it at the start and this encourages bad starts and consequent General Recalls. If it is more than one boat's length to leeward there is always the possibility that some boats will sail between it and the line and legally enable them to cross the line close to the committee boat.

RULES
Starting Line Marks

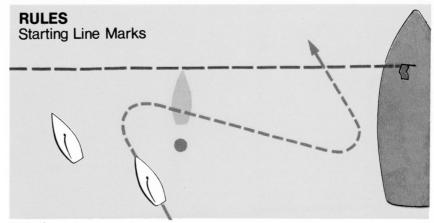

6.20 ▲

On some lines this could be a very big advantage. If there is less than one boat's length between the mark and the line it is illegal to do this (6.20).

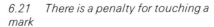
6.21 There is a penalty for touching a mark

6.22 Start and finish between Committee Boat and C. Marks A, B, C to be rounded to port—twice round

6.23 The red track is the incorrect rounding. The green track is the unwind plus the correct rounding

6.24 The green track is the penalty re-rounding. This re-rounding rule is in force unless the Sailing Instructions say not

6.25 Mark A to starboard, marks B and C to port. Both the red and the green tracks _leave_ mark A to starboard

6.26 At starting line marks the re-rounding must be outwards

6.27 Marks A, B, C, D to port. A may be ignored on the second leg when the boat may want to come inshore to avoid the strongest current

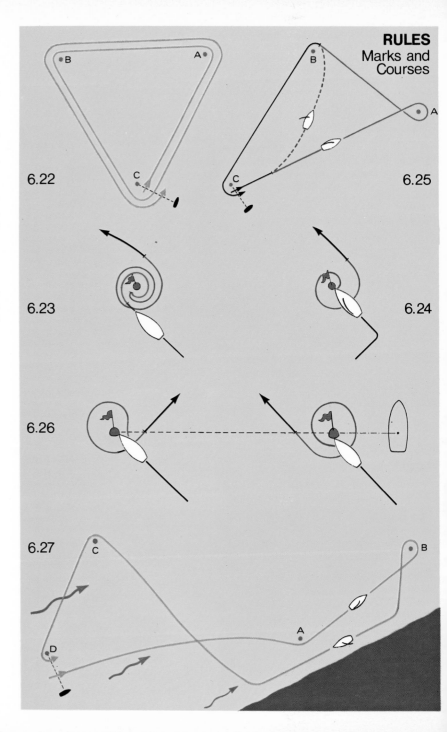

6.22

6.25

6.23

6.24

6.26

6.27

Sailing the course

The rules say that each mark has to be rounded or passed in succession so that a string following the boat's wake would enclose all the marks in the correct order (6.22). Thus, if a mark is rounded the wrong way, the course can only be corrected by unwinding the 'string' first (6.23).

Similarly, if the mark re-rounding penalty is in force (check with the Sailing Instructions), a boat which touches a mark (6.21) has to re-round that mark before continuing so that the 'string' would enclose the mark with one extra closed loop (6.24).

Committees sometimes purposely describe a course with a loop in it. This is a common trap since, unless the committee is very careful in wording the course, this mark can be effectively missed out (6.25). It has never been tested by Appeal but it is generally accepted that if the word 'rounding' is used then it means exactly that and a looped mark so described has to be rounded and not passed at a distance. However, a course which is displayed as a series of numbers or letters on a board (0.17 and 7.9) should not have looped marks unless two are enclosed in the loop. Then it is impossible to mis-interpret the intention.

Starting line marks, when touched, have to be re-rounded outwards; i.e. the starboard end clockwise; the port end counter clockwise (6.26).

As far as the racing rules are concerned marks only become involved if they are on the leg of the course the boat is sailing. Thus, from the preparatory signal until she has rounded the weather mark, the starting marks, the weather mark itself and any other mark which does not require the direct course to turn a corner, are marks which must not be touched and must be passed on the correct side and to which the 'string' rule applies.

After successfully rounding a mark all the previous marks can be completely ignored and rank only as obstructions while sailing the next leg of the course so that only marks on that leg then become relevant (6.27).

6.28 The anchor rope does not count as part of the mark. You can touch it but do not push off from it. That would be 'unfair propulsion'.

Ground tackle does not count as part of the mark so the boat in 6.28 is alright provided the crew does not *push* off which would be an 'Unfair means of propulsion' (see also page 24). Boats or other objects temporarily attached to a mark also rank only as obstructions and may be touched unless the Sailing Instructions say otherwise.

6.29   Key to the drawing
A   Gate Launch
B   Pathfinder
C   Guard Launch
D   Starting Mark
E   Committee Boat
F   Limit of Starting Line
G   Boats waiting to start

Distances:
A to B is about 3 lengths of B.
C is about 30 yards ahead and 10 yards to leeward of B for centreboard boats.
D to F is about 3 minutes sailing time for a large fleet.
Boats G sail as close as possible under the stern of A.
B turns at F and also passes astern of A. Boats G are not allowed to pass between A and B or B and C.

Gate starts

In some areas the Gate (or Rabbit) Start is used to send off a large fleet of one-designs. The drawing (6.29) shows the usual method and, providing the wind remains constant during the period that the pathfinder opens the gate, a remarkably level start will result. Frequently a very large part of the fleet will arrive at the windward mark together. Some say that this is in itself a disadvantage of the gate start because it simply transfers the congestion to the weather mark but if the windward leg is adequately long it will give enough opportunity for boats to sort themselves out.

A more interesting objection is that it takes most of the excitement out of starting. To the experienced competitor this method will certainly reduce the opportunity that he has for dealing with more than half the fleet at one move, but for the less experienced it gives an opportunity to start the first leg with no disadvantage on the experts.

The pathfinder is usually taken from the lower end of the top ten per cent of the fleet; i.e. eighth in the previous race in a fleet of eighty. There is an incentive for the pathfinder to sail as fast and as high as possible since, during the opening of the gate, she is racing against the early starters. The fastest boats will therefore normally start early and the slow ones will give themselves less time to lose distance on the leaders by starting late.

There are other advantages: previously planned race strategy is easier to carry out since there should be no interference at the start; all boats can start at the favoured starboard 'buoy' position in clear wind and, provided they can organise a small gap between themselves and the next astern, they can tack clear or carry on as they wish; fewer rules are likely to be broken; no-one can start too early; no-one need barge since the mark is itself moving.

On the other hand it is not so easy to marshal the boats into the correct starting area; the starboard limit of the line is not known with precision before the gate is open; in the event of failure, which includes interference with the pathfinder, it is not so easy to reorganise a new start.

If the wind is very shifty or light the method is not suitable since the gate may open faster or slower during its travel and may alter in direction too. Unlike a fixed line where, even if the wind does change, at least all the crews can see where it is, the gate, and hence the limits of the line, are not fixed until the gate is open and in very light winds it may never open at all.

Heavy winds are perfectly possible in theory but the committee and pathfinder may have difficulty in managing the necessary perfect sequence of operations in rough conditions.

In strong currents, the apparent wind effects, except those relating to the windward mark, are automatically cancelled out since the pathfinder and the competitors are all floating free. The only difficulty is the fixed mark at the port end which is usually anchored to the sea-bed. Thus, though the line may be crossed successfully initially, boats may still be unable to weather the port end mark. In cross currents the committee should lay the windward mark according to the same rules as for fixed lines discussed earlier.

The tactics for a gate start are to go late if you want to keep to the starboard side of the windward leg and to go early for the port side. Keep well up to the line in advance of the pathfinder and dive close under the committee boat's stern with as much speed as possible but beware of the boats close hauled to leeward. They do not have to give room at a 'starting mark'. It is dangerous to pace the pathfinder on port tack until you are ready to make your dive for the line because you have no right of way and your manoeuvring space is restricted.

With these reservations the gate is certainly a very successful alternative to the flying method especially for use on open water windward starts with a medium strength steady wind.

Transit lines

The most common method for club racing is to have a fixed transit on shore with one or more limit marks off shore (*6.30*). Sometimes there is provision for angling the line by moving the transit posts. Usually this means that the limit marks must be moved too.

Where there is very deep water just off shore as is found on rocky coasts or on mountain lakes and reservoirs the length of line may be unlimited but the fleet may have to pass on the shorewards side of a fixed mark a few hundred yards up the shore. This can call for finely judged positioning on the line and well thought out tactics at the mark if a clear getaway is to be ensured.

If the mark is to windward and has to be rounded to port (*6.31*) the perfect course would be a port tack into the shore then a starboard tack just to clear the mark. It is essential to do a dummy run beforehand and to note the point on the shore (A) that has to be reached before you are safe to go for the mark; failing to fetch it would be disastrous since you would have to go back onto port and approach without right-of-way (X). Do not allow yourself to be forced offshore by starboard tack boats (Y). Go under their sterns if necessary (Z) in order to reach your marked point.

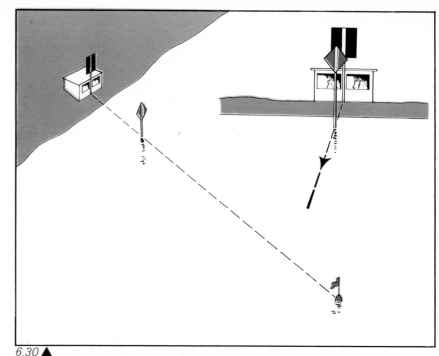

6.30 ▲

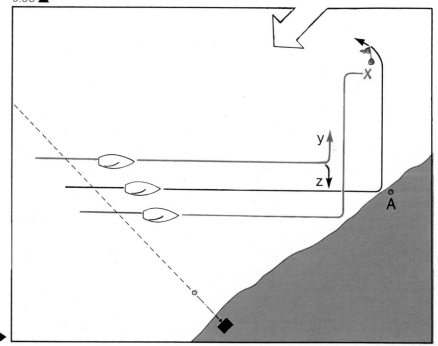

6.31 ▶

A starboard hand mark can be fetched in one starboard tack (*6.32*) but everyone will want to be at that one point on the line (A). Furthermore there are a number of traps to be avoided (see Part Three concerning tacking at marks and also overlaps at marks) and a committee would be very wise to lay it well offshore to avoid congestion and impossible right-of-way situations developing and if they do not want to be sitting at protest meetings well into the night.

Reaching starts on this type of line are very tricky to manage (*6.33*). Success depends on hitting the line with the gun at full speed and with the fastest possible course and distance combination (A). Your timing has to be perfect and if your mathematics are not up to it, a good approximation can be made after making some timing runs (see also *5.39*).

Trouble can arise at the mark owing to the sudden change over in right-of-way from the *Windward/Leeward* rule, where the leeward boat has the advantage (i.e. C over B), to a point two lengths from the mark where the *Room at marks* rule takes over and the rights are reversed (i.e. B over C in the positions shown). Immediately after the mark leading boats may be unable to tack owing to the rule which prevents a boat from *Tacking too close* to another. See the Appendix for further references and fuller explanation of the rules involved.

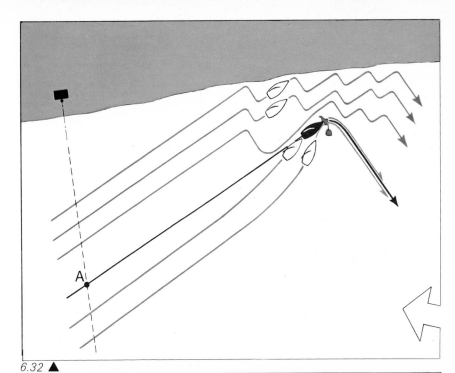

6.32 ▲

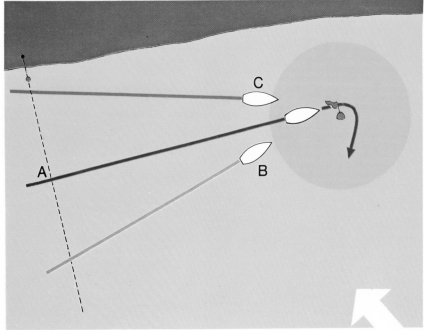

6.33 ▶

Open water lines

Apart from the transit line of un-limited length (6.34–A) many com-binations of buoys and committee boats are used, the commonest being a line between a moored committee boat or raft and a fixed buoy (B). There is usually a small inner distance mark which is not part of the line itself but ranks as a starting-line mark and which keeps boats away from the committee (C). Sometimes there is no inner limit mark. Sometimes there are two committee boats with inner limits at each end (D) which will be in radio contact and possibly with duplicated signals.

For helmsmen the most worrying problem is how to tell when one is almost on the line. With the transit line, especially if the end posts are good and high, it is quite easy to estimate one's distance from the line, but the small inconspicuous limit marks on an open-water line cannot be relied on as a transit and they are too easily obscured by other approaching boats (6.35).

The best answer is to find one's own back transit mark from amongst the background (6.36). This is not possible if the horizon is open sea with no prominent features but even then a cloud formation or a ship can be used for the last half minute that matters. Remember that the transit can be made through whichever end of the line has the most convenient back mark.

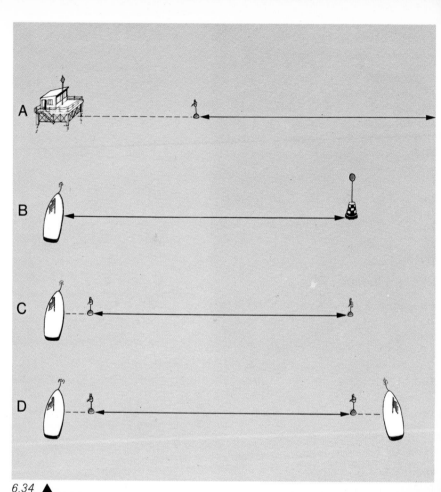

6.34 ▲

6.35 At the last moment the line be-comes obscured ▶

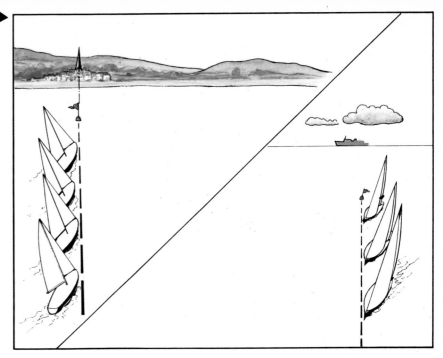

If it is impossible to fix up any sort of transit there is nothing for it except to estimate by eye how close one is. Obviously this is easier near either end but experience shows that the boats in the centre almost always hold back. They could usually approach much nearer to the line than they think they can (*6.14*). The only common exception to this is when there is some outside influence which pushes boats closer, such as a weather-going current. Then, if a small group of boats obscures the line, everyone else moves forward and the result is usually a general recall.

So-be bold! You may be surprised how often you will be right.

Transit bearings

Transits are unconsciously used all the time on the water. You will find after a while that you are automatically estimating your position relative to two other objects by noting their changing position, one behind the other.

There is a basic rule about transits which is of the greatest possible value when racing. If you are closing on an object, whether it is itself fixed or moving, look at the background behind it. If the *background* appears to move to the *right* of the object you will pass to the *right* also (*6.37*), and vice versa.

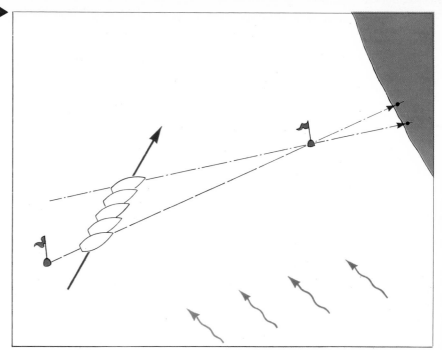

In *6.38* a current from the side pushes the boat off the direct line to the mark. Aiming off, as in *6.39*, brings a point on the background (X) steady with respect to the mark and a direct course over the ground results.

So this fact is used in two important ways:

● *Setting a course for the next mark.* If you can see that the background behind the mark is moving (*6.38*), steer to one side or other until the background remains steady (*6.39*). Then you know that, on that course, you have automatically allowed for current or leeway or both.

● *To know instantly if you will pass ahead or astern of another boat.* Watch the background—you will pass the same side as the background moves (*6.37*).

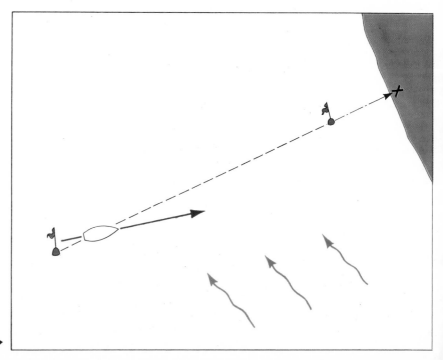

6.40 ▶

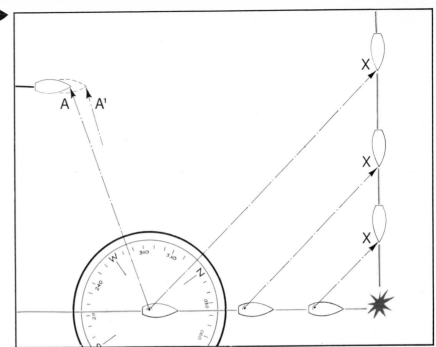

Steady bearings

In larger boats where a hand bearing compass can be used (*3.12*), the 'steady bearing' technique provides additional information. Repeated bearings on another boat (A) will tell you if she is gaining (A') or losing distance on your own boat or if she will cross ahead or astern (*6.40*). If the bearing remains steady she is not gaining, or there will shortly be a collision! (X)

Another use for this instrument is to find out how near one is to the lay-line to the weather mark. The critical bearing will have been worked out in the pre-start checks (340° in this case) and it is then only a matter of sighting on the mark and comparing the reading or of sighting along the bearing to see how far you have to go. Overstanding the weather mark is one of the commonest and easiest ways to lose a race but, if the error is spotted in time, one can at least minimise it by sailing free from the earliest moment (*6.41*).

When approaching a mark from some distance it is also essential to know the currents. Again, if there is only a flat horizon as background, repeated compass bearings will give the answer. At night this is almost the only reliable way of finding one's position relative to the mark which in such a case is normally a lit navigation buoy.

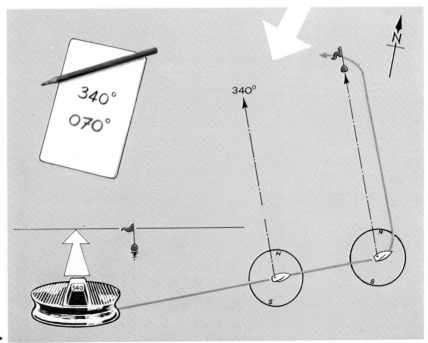

6.41 ▶

Part Three

The Race

To explain inter-boat tactics and how they are related to the racing rules in a way which is logical and real, we must think about a race from before the start until after the finish. We must consider an actual race in detail and see which rules control the various boat-to-boat situations which are commonly repeated in all races and how a crew can use these rules to develop some standard tactics.

There are some incidents which constantly recur and which will often cause a reaction in one boat which is a certain race loser. An example is after the start when one can see boats sailing for an amazing length of time in the foul air from a boat to windward and they are therefore losing distance every second. Another case is two boats meeting close-hauled on opposite tacks. The port tack boat will not bear away to pass under the stern of the starboard tacker because it instinctively feels like a defeat. So she tacks but is immediately 'run over' and 'killed stone dead' by the other.

The crew must learn, in the first case, to 'see the wind', which means to give ones mind a bird's eye view of the race so that it can visualise the relative positions of the boats and the airflow which is giving them motive power. The second case is an example of how one must always be thinking ahead.

7.1   The race

The race course key

Look at this diagram which shows many of the elements of a typical race (7.2). Keep it in your mind when you are studying the descriptions of the race and the analysis of possible incidents which can occur on various parts of the course. Use it to connect the discussions about the merits of this or that rule or tactical move with the reality of the race as a whole. Follow the coloured boats round the course and note the various incidents which will be discussed in more detail in the following chapters.

Never forget that the object of the race is to cross the finishing line first. What happens between the start and the finish is a battle of wits, expertise and boat handling techniques and it is the object of this book to help you to understand this complicated but fascinating game and be able to begin to play and enjoy it.

The boxed areas refer to later sections and provide a connecting reference which the reader may find helpful.

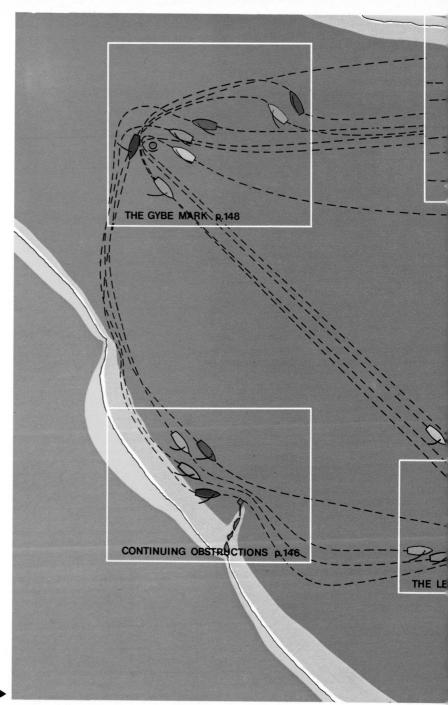

THE GYBE MARK p.148

CONTINUING OBSTRUCTIONS p.146

THE LE

7.2 ▶

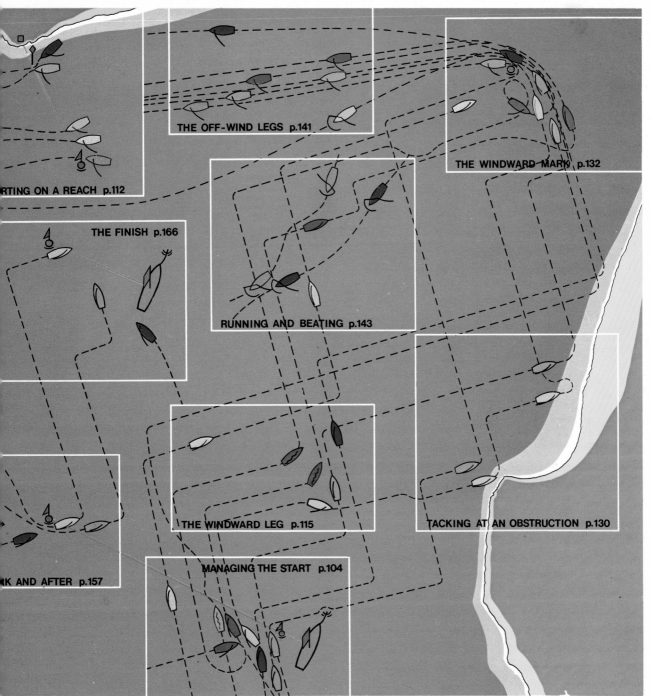

RTING ON A REACH p.112

THE OFF-WIND LEGS p.141

THE WINDWARD MARK p.132

THE FINISH p.166

RUNNING AND BEATING p.143

THE WINDWARD LEG p.115

TACKING AT AN OBSTRUCTION p.130

RK AND AFTER p.157

MANAGING THE START p.104

Chapter 7

Before the Start

Before going out to the start you should have made up your mind on the general strategy of the race but there is one more subject which can have a significant influence on this.

Points scoring

We have assumed until now that you are trying to win the race, but you may be more concerned with winning a series which could involve trying to avoid being covered and slowed down by the series leader or trying to cover a challenger to your own points lead. Before you go out to start you should have worked out the up-to-date points situation and, if it is the last race in a series, who can win and under what circumstances.

Points systems are of two main types—straight or loaded. In the former each place scores an equal number of points, usually one. In the latter the better placings receive a graded bonus. Sometimes this bonus extends in a graduated progression right to the end but the more commonly used Olympic system favours only the first six places.

There is no theoretical difference between the high- or low-point systems though the latter, which uses zero or one for the winner, is easier to administer and copes better with the points to be allocated to boats which retire or are disqualified. Sometimes there is an additional points penalty for boats disqualified after protest compared to boats voluntarily retiring while still on the course.

The other important feature is whether or not a discard is allowed. If the 'worst race' points can be dropped from the total it profoundly affects the running points situation since it cannot be known until after the last race which will be each competitor's worst.

There is some double-thinking about points systems today. Series racing was introduced in an effort to find a truer winner because it was thought that a single once-and-for-all result was too much subject to chance. This is a debatable point for a start since it depends how much trouble one is prepared to take in preparation but many people are so slapdash about their racing that it could be true for the majority whose views have prevailed. Nevertheless, a single championship race for the 'big prize' is probably the purest and most refined form of racing.

However, points series were introduced to reduce the effects of chance but then the cry was heard that this was not fair because one bad race could ruin a boat's chances! So one now has to allow a discard to reduce the effects of chance still more! Finally a loaded points system is introduced to favour the winners again!

Inevitably someone will complain that any system is unfair but nothing is unfair that is not compulsory. There are rules for any game. You enter the game under those rules and stick to them. If you do not like the rules either you do not take part or you start another game. The true tactical sailor will study the rules carefully and work out how he can make the most of them. So you should study the points system for this particular series and work out your tactics to win under these rules and not under the rules you think ought to have been used. This is perhaps the most useful piece of advice that can be given to anyone involved in a sport.

To illustrate the effects of different points systems look at these examples:

1 Using a straight low-point scoring system the points after 5 races are:

Him 1, 2, 6, 3, 14, ? = 26
(12 allowing a discard)
You 2, 1, 5, 6, 4, ? = 18
(12 allowing a discard)

In the last race if *You* finish lower than sixth you might allow *Him* to be one place higher and still win. This will leave *You* with level points.

But the various tie-breaking rules include 'who beat who most often' which would not solve the example above, or 'who had most wins, seconds and so on' which would give the series to *Him*. You will have to refer to the sailing instructions to find the particular one for this series.

So, in this example, if *You* finish sixth or worse in this last race you must also beat *Him* to retain the series.

2 In another more extreme but quite typical example, provided *He* finishes lower than eighth *You* will still win even if *You* retire:

Him 1, 1, 1, 6, 20, ? = 29
(9 allowing discard)
You 3, 4, 3, 2, 5, ? = 17
(12 allowing discard)

There is a chance here for really thorough and severe covering to push *Him* as far as possible down the fleet. However, it would not be 'fair sailing' to disable your opponent or push *Him* back by illegal means and then to retire yourself.

In this example if *He* finishes higher than eighth it becomes progressively worse for *You*. If *He* finishes fifth *You* have to be first to be sure of winning the series.

Loaded points systems complicate the arithmetic still more. Under Olympic scoring the points are shown in the table.

In the second example the scores would be:

Him 0, 0, 0, 11.7, 26, ? = 37.7
(11.7 with discard)
You 5, 7, 8, 5.7, 3, 10, ? = 32.4
(22.4 with discard)

Now, if *You* win you can only beat *Him* overall if he is sixth. If *You* were third *He* would have to be eleventh or lower for *You* to be safe. A much more severe task.

Your strategy therefore depends on the system. With a loaded points system it is much more important to go for wins than to be consistently near the front, contrary to what is generally believed.

Olympic Points Scoring System

Notes: Based on a seven race series—one discarded, or if necessary a series of six or five races—one discarded in each case but never less than five.
Boats which did not compete (DNC) in that race, which did not start (DNS), which failed to finish or which retired voluntarily (RET), or which were subsequently disqualified (DSQ), score points for a finishing place equal to the number of series entrants plus one. Ties are broken in favour of the boat with the most first places (or second places etc.).

Place:	1st	2nd	3rd	4th	5th	6th	7th etc.
Points:	0	3	5.7	8	10	11.7	place + 6

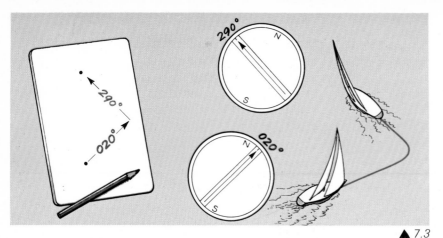

▲ 7.3

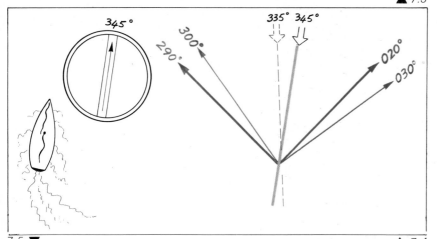

7.5 ▼

▲ 7.4

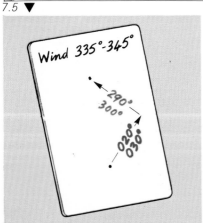

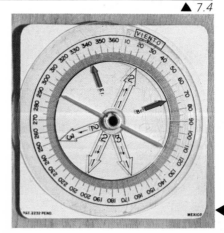

◀ 7.6 *A simple calculator for 90°*
triangular courses

Pre-start checks

We have studied at some length the type of motive power that can be expected during the race and this governs the sails to be used, the way the boat is tuned and the general way that the course should be ideally covered. It may by now have become obvious that for this race it is best to keep to the starboard side after the start and so this will affect the way the start itself is made. In such a case for example it might be best to start near the starboard end of the line so that it would be easier to tack onto port soon without too much interference.

There are still a number of checks to be made, partly to confirm the weather pattern and the race strategy but also to establish the course as exactly as possible. No time must be lost during the race in looking for marks in the wrong place nor in hoisting the spinnaker on the wrong side nor in setting off from the lee mark on the unfavourable tack. It is vital to *know* these things beforehand.

Using the compass and noteboard (see also *5.21*), the list of pre-start mechanical checks, not all of which will be needed in every type of race, is as follows:

1   Arrive in the start area early. Set up the boat for top speed to windward in the prevailing conditions, which is essential if the

results of the following measurements are to mean anything.

2 Sail to windward on both tacks. Note down the headings on each tack (7.3).

3 Put the boat carefully head to wind and note the wind direction (7.4). Check it against the headings on each tack and, if there is a discrepancy, discover why, i.e. there was a wind shift or perhaps waves were causing better speed and pointing on one tack. Try to find the rhythmic pattern if there is one and note this down too (7.5).

4 Discover which end of the start line is nearer to windward (7.7). The committee may have set the line square to the bearing of the weather mark (330°) which would be wrong in this case. They may also have purposely given it some bias. Sail exactly along the line with the mainsail trimmed until the battens only are drawing and the foresail is fully eased. Then sail the other way without touching the mainsheet setting. If more of the sail is now drawing the windward end is behind you and vice versa (7.8). Compass bearings are often not possible owing to the line being obscured or other boats getting in the way.

5 Immediately check the wind direction again and relate the angle of the start line to the rhythmic wind shift pattern. Is

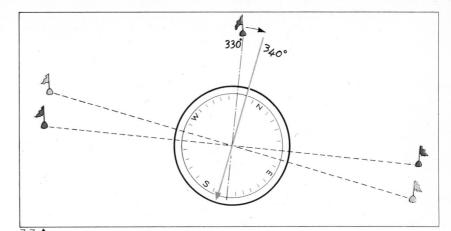

7.7 ▲

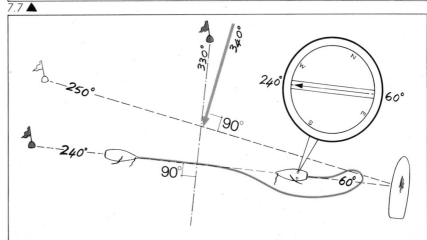

7.8 ▲

7.9 Diamond buoy (port), buoy A ▶ (port), buoy K (port). Three laps. Windward mark bears 270°.

101

one end even more favoured on the next shift or does the balance move to the other end?

6 Check on the course. By this time it may be ten minutes to the start and the committee should have set the course and be able to give the compass bearing of the first mark (7.9). Try to spot the mark. A small disc calculator (7.6) is useful in all these operations.

7 Check the current by looking at anchored marks or mark boats (7.10).

8 On your already prepared noteboard mark .in the windward mark and the courses between marks and adjust for current if significant (7.11 & 3.6).

9 Set up the spinnaker gear on the correct side for the first hoist (7.12).

10 Check the wind direction again and have a moment's thought about everything. Look at the sky, look at your note-board and decide finally which end of the line to start and which side of the course to go for.

11 At some time during the pre-start period time a run along the line. This will give you a basis for your final run-up to the start but remember that it always takes longer in the end owing to interference.

12 Five-minute gun! Check the timing. Tidy the boat. Bail out water. Check for weed on centreboard and rudder. A final check on the tuning. A final check on wind direction. Get into position for your run up to the start.

▲ 7.10

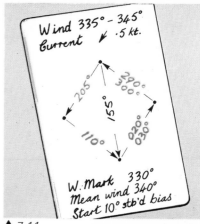

▲ 7.11

Course calculators

The simple type of course calculator shown in *7.6*, if *set to the wind direction*, can immediately give the theoretical lay-lines to the windward mark (the same as the tacking angles) and also the theoretical angles for the starting line. The amount of bias on the line and the actual direction of the windward mark can be written down on the deck or the note-board. The difference between the latter and the true wind indicates whether the spinnaker can be set on the reaching legs and on which side.

On an Olympic course it also gives the compass bearings of the marks if the pointer is *re-set to the windward mark* bearing.

A more sophisticated calculator (*7.13*) has two revolving discs and a base board. The advantages here are that the windward mark bearing and the true wind direction can both be set at the same time. Not only that, the actual tacking angles can be noted. It also gives the correct gybe for the running leg, and thus largely dispenses with the need for a note-board.

Grid compasses can also be marked up to show much of this information and have the additional advantage of indicating, via the needle or compass card, exactly when you are sailing on a lift or a heading slant (*5.21*).

◀ *7.12 Can the spinnaker be carried on the first reach? Or the second? And on which side?*

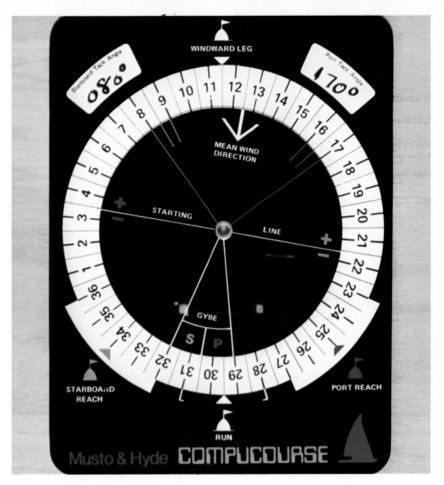

7.13 A more elaborate course calculator with two discs

Chapter 8

Managing the Start

When sailing a Finn single-hander internationally I sometimes found that I sailed much faster and had better results when I left the beach late and arrived in the starting area just as the gun was about to fire and charged headlong straight across the line. The anxiety not to be late undoubtedly set the adrenalin going and the necessary 'killer instinct' was well developed too so that aggressive tactics became automatic and were often successful. This type of start is not to be recommended though; apart from the timing being too chancy it is only likely to work if the course is well known.

8.1 *An area championship for Mirror dinghies*

When sailing with a crew of six others in a One-Tonner I had to discipline myself to be thorough in preparation and practical in carrying out planning. Things happen more slowly but once started are impossible to correct in an instant as can be done in the Finn dinghy. The manoeuvre had to be right first time and, for a dinghy sailor, the anxiety was often acute as I watched the winch grinding in the genoa sheet while the yacht slowly gathered speed and momentum (8.3).

A really outstanding start can win a race there and then (0.9). A bad start can mean that there is very little chance of good placing. It is absolutely vital to get away with a clear wind and top boat-speed. Every second that passes after the gun and before the line is crossed is multiplied many times in your accumulated deficit on the leaders. The same goes for sailing in another boat's wind-shadow—every second that passes the leaders are getting further out of

reach. The aim is to cross the line just after the gun with top speed and in the right position. Very easily said but not so easily done. However the techniques can be learnt and there is no reason at all why a reasonably good start should

8.2 A world championship start for Solings

8.3 Grinding in the genoa on a big offshore racer is a team job

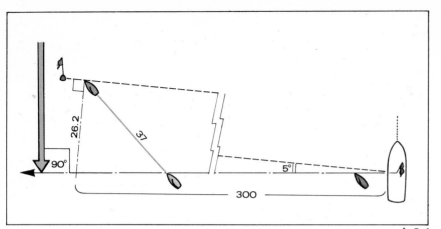

▲ 8.4

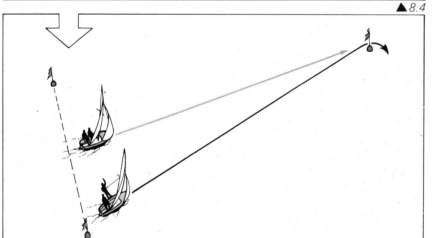

▲ 8.5

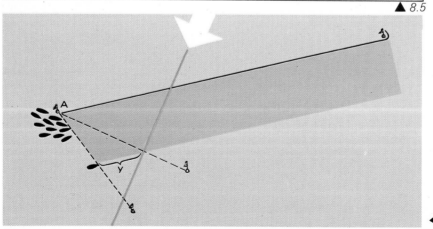

not be completely normal. Look at this detailed advice and then practise on the water. A little experience will soon give confidence and your results will improve greatly.

Managing the start correctly comes under four main sub headings as follows:

- The geometry
- The strategy
- The rules
- The tactics and techniques

The geometry

First get the geometry right. Unless the line is perfectly laid one end will be more favourable than the other. If it is a windward start, one end will be further to windward. Find out which either by comparing the wind direction with the angle of the line or by the reaching method (7.8). The former gives a reading which can be converted approximately into distance; the latter is only comparative but is usually all that is required.

As an example take a line 300 yards long angled so that the port end is favoured by 5°. It is quite usual for Race Committees to give such a bias intentionally in order to encourage boats to spread along the line rather than risk them bunching at the more popular starboard end. However 5° is easily detectable on the compass so those in the know will certainly favour the port end. You should be there too.

◀ 8.6

The port end is approximately (300×sin 5°) yards nearer the wind, i.e. 26.2 yards (*8.4*). But boats travel at about 45° to the wind when beating and so to be this much further to windward a boat would be $\sqrt{2} \times 26.2$ yds ahead (i.e. 37 yds) on a close-hauled course, or over seven lengths for a 470. What a distance to give away at the start!

A great deal of racing is done on fixed courses from fixed start lines and the first mark may not be to windward. Again, work out the geometry. If the mark is to windward of the line, but you can fetch it quite easily in one tack from the more leeward end, it usually pays to start to leeward (*8.5*). Not only will this end be nearer but modern boats usually are faster when sailing slightly free than when further off the wind and there are better tactical possibilities too (see also *5.37* and 'The Windward Leg').

If the mark can not be quite fetched a mistake is often made by Race Committees in setting the line square to the course to the first mark rather than square to the wind that is being felt by the free-floating competitors. Look out for this common error. It will mean that there is only one place to start (A) and in a hot fleet nearly everyone will be there (*8.6*). Starting further down the line means you are giving away the extra distance 'y'. If it is a running start with a current (*8.7*) you have to think ahead to what is going to happen at the first mark. The pure geometry of the start line is of much smaller importance than

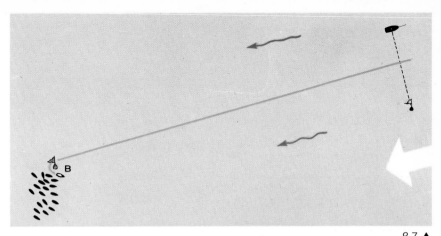

8.7 ▲

the positioning of the boat at this mark which, in a light wind, might best be rounded last to gain the windward position on the following windward leg (B).

The strategy

The example just mentioned shows how strategy overlaps with tactics. The former might be said to be a long term version of tactics. By the latter we are thinking of close-quarters manoeuvres. Thus the general strategy of the race has already been decided but how do you put it into practice?

The strategic options at the start are as follows:

1 After the start—work over to the port side of the course.
2 After the start—work over to starboard.
3 Cover a specific opponent.
4 Avoid being covered by a specific opponent.
5 All or nothing— if it is vital to get a good start.
6 Play safe—if it is vital to avoid trouble.

It is also self evident that whatever the type of start the 'golden rules' of racing will always apply:

● Fight for CLEAR AIR
● Go for TOP BOAT SPEED
● THINK AHEAD
● AVOID TROUBLE

plus one more:

● Retain FREEDOM OF MANOEUVRE

Therefore the actual positioning of the boat at the start must not only enable the strategy to be carried out but must ensure that these 'golden rules' are fulfilled immediately the gun fires.

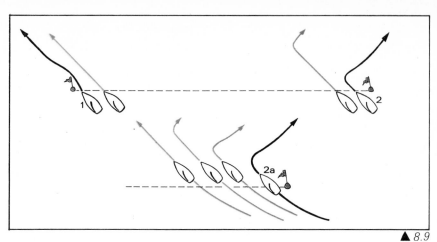

8.8　A boat gets clear at the port end of the start line but there is no way out for 20302!

▲ 8.9

So from the strategic viewpoint 1. will be satisfied by starting near the port end with freedom to sail free and obtain clear air to leeward and ahead of the fleet (8.8 & 8.9— 1).

2. will need a start at the starboard end with freedom to tack or otherwise manoeuvre the boat over to the starboard side of the fleet (2).

In windward starts it often pays to go late in order to be sure of being able to tack away. (2a).

3. and 4. mean that the respective opponent must be watched all the time, at least from the preparatory signal, and appropriate tactical action taken.

the best position at all costs such as a port tack start (8.10–5a), diving in from the windward side (5b) or starting from 'coffin corner' (5c).

6. requires either a late start or one in a thinly populated part of the line.

▼ 8.10

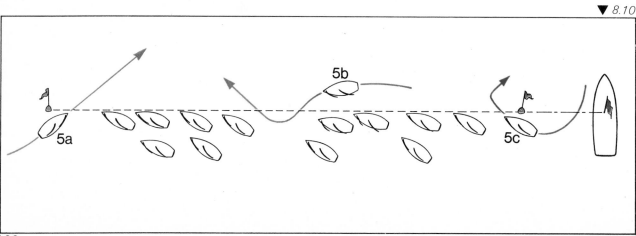

The rules

The main rules applicable to the start are as follows (*8.11*) and all rules begin to operate from the preparatory signal (usually the five-minute gun). *Refer also to the Appendix for their full names and numbers*:

1 *Starboard tack has right of way* and so normally the run-up to the start should be made on starboard tack so that there is one less thing to think about (1).

2 *Windward yacht keeps clear* This has a useful tactical application in the last few seconds before the gun as we shall see (2).

3 But, *luffing before clearing the starting line* must only be done slowly, and if your mainmast is aft of the windward yacht's helmsman, you can only luff as far as close-hauled (3a). Apart from straightforward boat-to-boat effects this means that you cannot, in such a case, squeeze up to round the port end mark by luffing above close-hauled if this affects the windward boat (3b and *8.8*). Remember that there is no 'proper course' before a yacht has cleared the starting line (see page 117) and so you can luff slowly head to wind if you wish provided your mast is ahead of the windward boat's helmsman. Therefore, on a reaching start, boats can claim room at the leeward end mark when approaching from leeward (3c) but must turn to their 'Proper Course' immediately after starting if they don't have luffing rights (page 117).

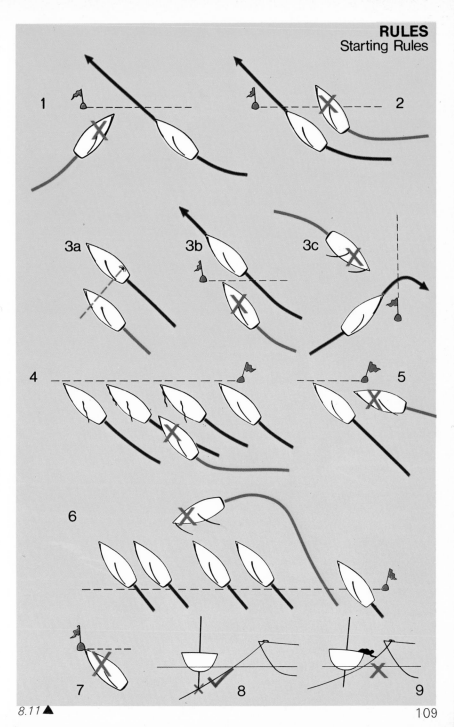

8.11 ▲

◀ 8.12 Overtaking boat keeps clear!

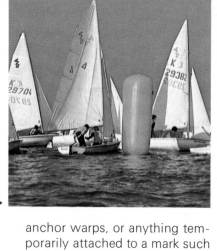

8.13 No barging at a starting mark! ▶

4 *Overtaking yacht keeps clear*
You must not run into the stern of a yacht which is hovering slowly just behind the line (4).

5 *No barging* at a starting line mark which has open water round it. The rules change significantly as the start is signalled, but to begin with just remember that approaching the end mark to pass to leeward of it, sailing either free of close-hauled or on a course below that to the first mark, whichever is appropriate, is dangerous. This is

called 'barging' and you have no rights to room.

6 Being *over the line* at the starting signal means that you have to return completely behind the line and re-start. Whilst doing this you have *no rights* and must not interfere with any other yacht.

7 *Starting line marks* must not be touched. The committee boat may or may not be a mark and the definition of the starting line given in the Sailing Instructions should be studied. Note that

anchor warps, or anything temporarily attached to a mark such as a dinghy or tender, are not parts of the mark and can be touched without penalty (8). Do not hang on to such objects or fend off from them unless compelled to or you may run into trouble with the rule controlling 'Means of Propulsion' (9).

▼ 8.14

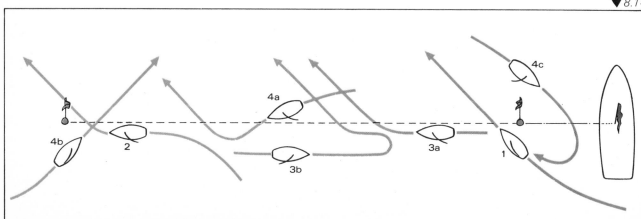

The tactics and techniques

The basic method is to time a run in advance from a suitable position to the particular point on the line where you want to start and then begin your run at 'starting time minus run time'. This seldom works without modification because other boats interfere (8.21 and 8.22). For the same reason, laying a close-hauled course to shave the starboard end mark from some distance away is bound to fail. You will end up some way down the line and very late. As with all things to do with racing the answer is to compromise and to leave as many options open for as long as possible.

The types of start which can be made are few and can be listed (8.14):

1 Starboard (or windward) end starts from a run-in as close to 'barging' as you can get away with (1).
2 Port (or lee) end starts which need careful timing to avoid running out of line before the gun goes (2).
3 Central starts which break into two variations:
   a) slowly approaching from the starboard end while trying to open up a hole to leeward (3a).
   b) approaching from the port end on a port reach and tacking into a clear space (3b).
4 Opportunist starts which are all relatively dangerous and include:

a) hovering to windward of the line and dropping with full speed into a clear hole in the last few seconds (4a).
b) port tack starts which can sometimes be spectacularly successful when made at the port end mark (4b).
c) diving from the windward side into 'coffin corner' (4c).

Starts in the types 1 to 3 need very careful control of the boat's speed during the approach which is usually made more or less slowly. In the last half minute you will either find that you are very close to the line and need to hover nearly stationary or you are in the second row and need to break through into the front. Very different tactics are needed.

In the first case the boat must be luffed which has the dual effects of slowing it down and of opening up a space to leeward (8.15). In the final few seconds you bear away into this specially created hole,

accelerate and shoot across the line with good speed (orange course).

Unfortunately there are several snags. First, your luff may take you over the line. Second, when you have opened up the space to leeward, a boat from astern may thankfully dive into it.

You may also be in the reverse position of being luffed over the line (8.16) and you will have to wriggle out of this as best you can. You may be able to reverse momentarily by backing the jib or you can drop to leeward by raising the centreboard but also remember that it is very difficult to sight your position relative to the line accurately. Normally you will not be as close to the line as you think you are so don't panic too soon. Also, the committee may not be able to see you due to other boats being in the way, so all is not necessarily lost.

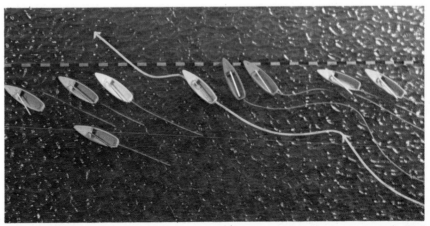

8.15 ▶

▲ 8.16

The filling up of your leeward hole is hard to prevent but can be discouraged by making several luffing sweeps as you approach (8.15). The disturbed wind in your wake and your erratic course should cause overtaking boats to drop a few extra yards to leeward and may force windward boats over the line.

Conversely, approaching from the second (or third) row needs more aggressive tactics. The weaving approach is also helpful in keeping a wider strip of water open but it won't get you through the solid ranks ahead. You cannot push into a gap by luffing because you will lose speed and manoeuvrability and be a sitting duck for a slow luff from a leeward boat. You

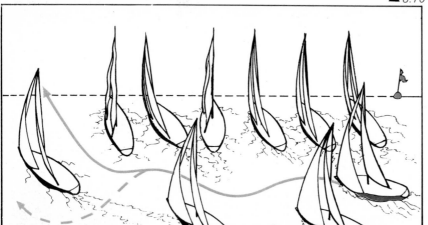

◀ 8.17

8.19 ▶

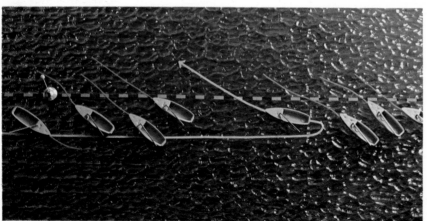

◀ 8.18

8.20 (far right) ▶

have to make continual dives under the sterns of those ahead until a gap of sufficient size appears (*8.17*).

Your main weapon is boat-speed and this is your only means of getting out of trouble. *Over-taking boat keeps clear* and so you have to use your speed to dive through to leeward. *Windward boat keeps clear* and so you must shoot across the bows of the nearly stationary hovering boats thus zig-zagging your way through the fleet. If you can do this at least you will have speed when the gun goes and can often get through a gap into clear air, even coasting through a boat's lee.

Often the fleet will bunch leav-ing quite large clear gaps. If your pre-race strategy tells you that the line is reasonably fair, then try the port reach approach. Tack just to leeward of a bunch leaving space to leeward of you to accelerate away. In spite of the approach on port tack this is often the safest and most reliable method of starting (*8.18*). It has the merit of a leeward start with space to leeward so that you can sail free and fast without the danger of running out of room in the last moments before the gun.

On a reaching start the main problem is whether to start to windward or to leeward. Unless race strategy dictates otherwise, a lee end start is often best but it does need very careful timing and the line must be crossed at full speed to avoid being blanketed and overrun by boats to windward (*8.19*). As has been described be-fore, the leeward boat is pointing higher and her speed brings her apparent wind further forward and clear of the other boats to wind-ward.

From a strict racing rule point of view a boat can approach the line from the wrong side close-hauled on starboard tack and, whilst forc-ing everyone else to keep clear, herself gain the key position at the 'gun' (*8.20*). But racing, like poli-tics, is to a great extent the art of the possible. It is no use standing on your rights if you are inevitably going to be swept away by a horde of advancing port tackers who will never have *time to respond*. I saw a

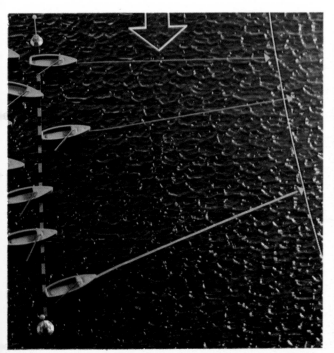

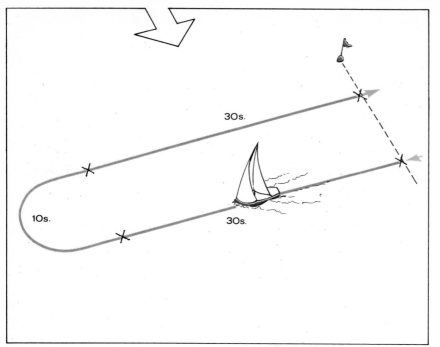

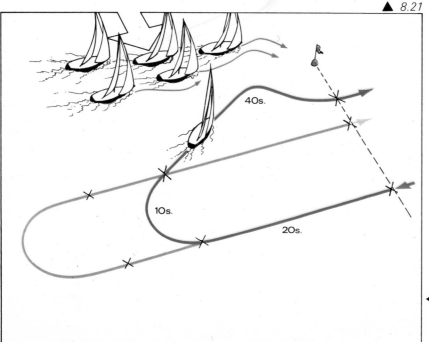

12-foot National dinghy try to do this once in a fleet of 150 boats and it ended up swamped, the crew swimming, the mast broken and floorboards and gear floating all around. She certainly had right-of-way but it did her no good at all. The race was lost and so was the series!

The most reliable method is to time a run, starting on the line in the reverse direction, sail for say 30 seconds, tack—10 seconds, sail back—30 seconds, making 70 seconds in all (8.21). If there is a current, timing will have to be adjusted. A 30 second sail away from the line could mean a three minute sail back which might be too long for accuracy.

The plan must be capable of being modified instantly. In example 8.22 if it becomes obvious that the tack will put you to leeward of a group of other boats, tack early, then luff. This will increase the time for the return run which is necessary and also force the windward boats to luff and slow down. Then bear away to cross the line with maximum speed. You should be able to get away best since you hold the initiative.

◀ 8.22

9.1 Try not to get involved in a tense duel for supremacy like this

Chapter 9

The Windward Leg

In the fight to get clear after the start it is only too easy to forget the next objective—the weather mark. Often the situation is that virtually the whole fleet is on starboard tack striving to gain that little extra speed which will win the duel with next door neighbours. Pairs of boats can sail for long periods as if locked together each trying to outpace the other (*9.1*). This is no way to win a yacht race!

Remember the Golden Rule—THINK AHEAD. You must not lose from your mind the next mark and your pre-race strategy. You must not allow yourself to get pinned down by other boats. You must retain FREEDOM OF ACTION (*9.2*).

9.2 Lasers exchange positions like chess pieces as they work the windward leg

The start should have been planned so that you can either sail free and fast to the port side (port end start) or so that you can tack over towards the starboard side (starboard end start). But owing to all the other boats which are trying to do the same thing the chances of being completely free to carry out your plan unobstructed are small. So what do you do?

The possible situations after the start are as follows:

a) You have your nose in front of a boat on your weather quarter (*9.3*).
b) You have your nose in front of a boat to leeward (*9.4*).
c) You are losing on a boat to windward (*9.4*).
d) You are losing on a boat to leeward (*9.3*).

a) and b) are potentially good situations but you have no freedom of action until you have resolved the duel. However the chances of a quick solution are good. If you are ahead and to leeward the lee-bowing effect will begin to affect the airflow over your opponent's sails (*9.3*–a). Squeeze up for a quick kill but make sure that you can do it fast. Pinching up slows you down and other boats to windward may start to over-run the pair of you.

To 'kill' a boat to leeward you need to sail free and fast to cover

116

her with your wind-shadow but you need to take care! *Windward yacht keeps clear* and so wait until you are certain that you have got her just on the edge of your blanketing zone (red line) before bearing away very slightly (*9.4*–b). The effect will be immediate and satisfying. Your opponent will drop back in disarray, windless and demoralised. She will certainly tack clear when she can and you can then decide whether to tack as well but your mind should by now have returned to the next mark. That is

9.3 ▼

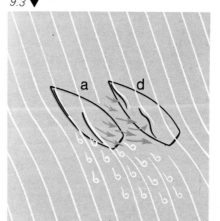

your first priority.

c) and d) are potentially bad. The tactic for d) is to tack if possible but in both cases you must act fast and with great precision, and, if the worst happens and you are trampled on, you must escape and think hard how to retrieve your lost distance.

The defence for c) is simply to sail free and fast. Keep your wind clear at all costs (*9.4*). There is not always room to sail free owing to

9.4 ▼

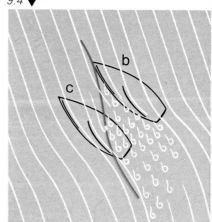

other leeward boats in which case there is nothing to be done but hope the windward boat will tack away. The dividing line between a clear wind and the edge of the wind-shadow is sharp (red line). The wind speed also increases slightly near the edge of this zone but it also comes from slightly more ahead. So be prepared to sheet in and flatten your sails when this happens—but not too much. Normally boats tend to sheet in too hard at the start and as a result kill their speed just at the moment when maximum speed is most needed.

Tactically, there is one other alternative but, though it may possibly knock out an opponent, it must have a disturbing effect on speed and concentration at a critical period in the race and so is not generally to be advised. This is to *luff* hard and try to hit the windward boat.

Luffing, Mast Abeam, Proper Course, Bearing Away

Here the rule about *luffing* must be explained in more detail. It also brings up the term *'proper course'* and the commonly heard hail of *'Mast Abeam!'* and also leads on to the rule about *'bearing away'*.

We said that before clearing the starting line, a leeward yacht may only luff slowly. After starting a boat with *luffing rights* can luff as hard and as suddenly as she pleases and is entitled to try to touch the windward boat (*9.5*–A).

9.5 ▶

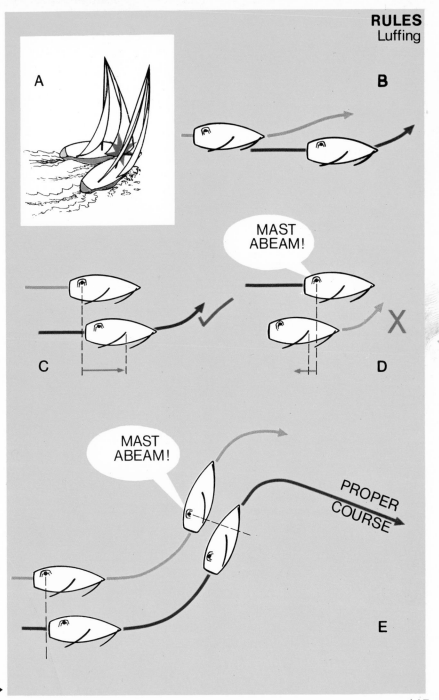

9.7 *Each of these three boats is overlapping the others but the leeward one has no luffing rights over the middle boat*

Luffing rights apply to a yacht which is clear ahead of another (B), or to a leeward yacht which is far enough forward of the other for her mast to be ahead of the windward yacht's helmsman (C). This is the critical 'mast abeam' position where luffing rights cease to apply and is the reason why, when the windward helmsman reaches this

▼ 9.6

position, he loudly hails 'Mast Abeam!' to establish a new rule situation (D).

If you are luffing, even slowly, and the helmsman of a boat to windward hails 'Mast Abeam!' you must immediately turn back on to your 'proper course' (E). Your luffing rights are gone as long as that overlap lasts. Luffing rights can only be regained by breaking the overlap and re-establishing it from ahead of 'Mast Abeam'.

Overlaps (9.6 — a), by definition in the rules, can only apply to boats on opposite tacks when they are rounding a mark or obstruction. They are broken in five ways (9.6):
b) One boat draws clear ahead.
c) One boat drops clear astern.
d) The boats diverge until there is more than two lengths of clear water between them.
e) One or both boats tack.
f) One or both boats gybe.

Proper Course is a term used in several rules and its meaning must be clearly understood. The definition in the rules says that it is '. . . any course which a yacht might sail after the starting signal, in the absence of the other yacht or yachts affected, to finish as quickly as possible.'

Points to remember are:
a) You are only required to sail a 'proper course' if other boats are affected and if a rule concerning proper course is involved.
b) For any boat there may be a

RULES Overlaps

a

b

c

d

e

f

number of possible 'proper courses' all of which might be justifiable.

c) The criterion for a 'proper course' is *not* that it *afterwards* proved to be the fastest course but that, *at the time*, there was a good reason for believing that it could be the fastest course.

So, if someone disputes whether you returned to your true proper course, after losing your luffing rights for example, you would have to think of a good reason for justifying sailing that course, i.e. perhaps you knew that the tide was more favourable inshore, or that there was a wind-shift approaching under a cloud on that side etc. In *9.8* both the red and green courses might be proper courses.

The definition goes on to say that there can be no proper course before the starting signal. However, after the starting signal and before clearing the starting line, the *Luffing before starting* rules still apply:

a) Luffs must be slow.
b) Even though a yacht is astern of the mast abeam position she can still force a windward yacht to luff up to a close-hauled course but no higher (*9.9*).

This last point is tactically useful if you have to cover a single opponent since you may be able to force her over the starting line early and gain a big advantage. A very important tactic in team or match racing too.

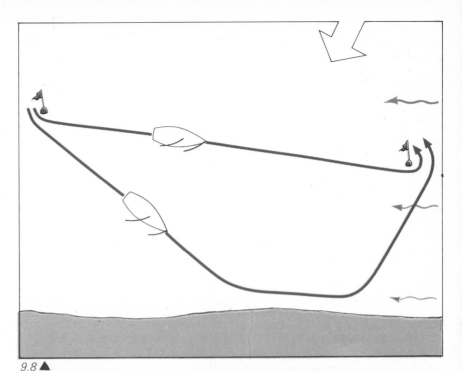

9.8 ▲

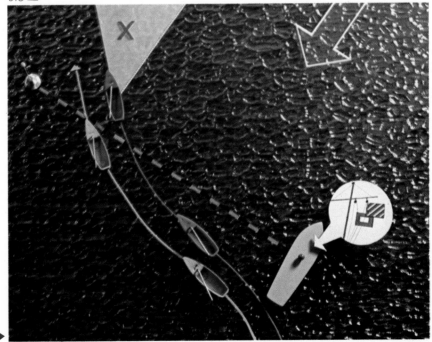

9.9 ▶

To sum up—after starting the tactics are:

● If yours is the windward boat—hail 'Mast Abeam!' as soon as the helmsman becomes level with the leeward boat's mast.

● If yours is the leeward boat—turn back to a 'proper course' the moment you hear a hail of 'Mast Abeam!'. Protest later if you think it unjustified.

If you are going to luff a windward boat do so hard and do so early. If left too late you will lose your luffing rights the moment the luff is started.

Finally the opposite to luffing—*bearing away*. When sailing on a *windward* leg (i.e. a close-hauled leg on which a boat will have to change tacks to reach the next mark) a yacht may sail as free as she likes but cannot force a leeward yacht to alter course (*9.10*).

The problem is to decide where the change-over point lies between 'forcing' and 'persuading'. Obviously it is never good to sail in another boat's wind-shadow. Therefore a windward boat could sail free and fast to place herself directly upwind of an opponent (A). Then the leeward boat would have to try to escape by sailing free herself (B) or by tacking away. But if you bear away so close to another yacht that she is forced to bear away to avoid touching then you will be wrong under the Wind-

9.12 Close covering on the windward leg ▶

120

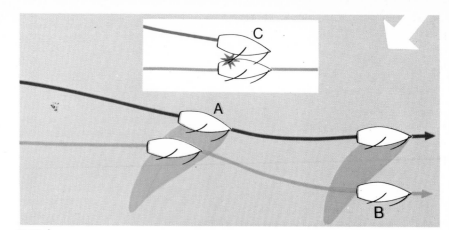

9.10 ▲

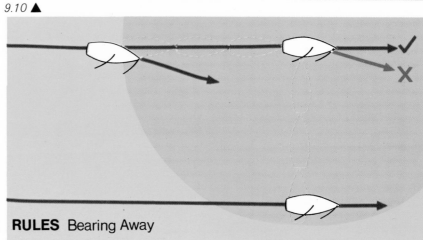

RULES Bearing Away

9.11 ▲

ward/Leeward rule (C). You would have initiated the action and so the onus of proof will be on you. Therefore use this tactic with care!

On a free leg of the course the rule is different and proper course becomes involved. You are not allowed to bear away below your proper course when there is another yacht within three lengths to leeward or within three lengths astern if she is steering to pass to leeward (*9.11*). It is easy to forget this rule and so if, when reaching, you find yourself shouted at it could well be on account of this.

Same-tack tactics

These rules, together with the Windward/Leeward rule, govern the tactics for boats sailing on the same tack. On a windward leg the advantage is mostly with the leader and this is especially so when boats are sailing on the same tacks (*9.12*). There are three main tactics all of which are for the defence of the position of a leading boat:

a) Covering—from a position to windward or ahead (*9.12–9.13*).
b) Lee-bowing—from a position ahead and to leeward (*9.3*).
c) Luffing—from a position to leeward or ahead (*9.5*).

The first two make use of interference with the other boat's wind supply. Luffing is a move to catch the other crew unawares and to take advantage of the confusion it causes.

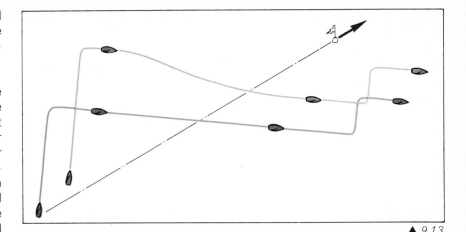

▲ *9.13*

▲ *9.14*

Covering

Immediately after the start the utmost priority for the first few minutes is full speed and a clear wind. Then, if you are lucky and find yourself leading a group of boats, or even the whole fleet, you must think about covering.

There is a Golden Rule for this which is disregarded at one's peril:

● Keep between your opponent and the next mark

This does not necessarily mean that you should keep slavishly on the exact line between the boat astern and the mark, tacking exactly when she does. It does mean keeping in the general upwind area not letting her escape to one side with the chance of picking up a better wind or current (*9.13*).

Covering one boat is not too difficult but try not to place yourself immediately upwind of her because this is simply asking her to tack away. What you should do is try to control her. Thus if you want her to continue on the same tack, you place your wind-shadow slightly behind her (*9.14*–Green). If you want her to change to the other tack you make it difficult for her to get wind by going slightly ahead (yellow). She cannot free off because of your wind-shadow and she is being slowed by your back-wind and so she tacks. She has no option.

Herding

This principle, which is called 'herding', is the extension of covering to control several boats at the same time.

It often happens that it is vital to keep in touch with the whole group of boats just astern. If you are preoccupied in covering one boat the others may escape. So herd the second boat towards the same direction as the third is going (*9.15*–a and b). By timing your tacks carefully (c) or by freeing off and sailing fast to adjust the effect of your wind-shadow you can persuade the second boat to herd the third and even go further than this sometimes.

The technique involves tacking early on a crossing boat if one wants her to tack back (*9.16*), and tacking late if one wants her to continue (*9.17*). By letting her get slightly ahead of your wind-shadow it makes her feel she has a chance of breaking clear, which of course she has not, because you keep her in position by controlling

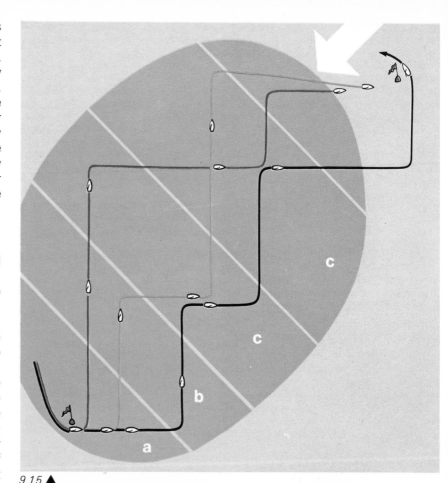

9.15 ▲

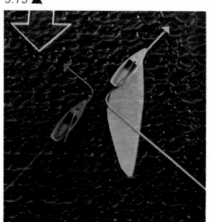

9.16 ▲

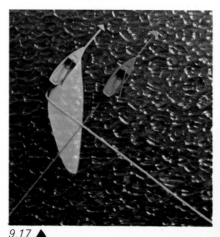

9.17 ▲

your own speed and pointing angle carefully.

It is seldom possible to extend control very far but, particularly in the later stages of a race, it is a very satisfactory tactic and causes worry in the minds of the opposing helmsmen which in turn gives them little chance of beating you. Psychologically, herding is an excellent technique and victims often fail to realise what is happening.

Breaking cover

Think now of yourself in the opposite position. One way of breaking cover is to 'pull the leader back' (*9.19*). This method is for use when you are being very closely covered and depends for its success on very smooth and faultless boat handling.

Remember that in a close-covering duel you, the covered boat, are really in control. You can tack on every slight heading windshift, turning smoothly so that you lose as little speed as possible (*9.19*). Your opponent has to follow you but is always slightly late and turns more sharply because you give no warning of your tack (a). You gain on each header and you gradually close the gap. Your opponent gets more nervous and jumpy the closer you get, his technique deteriorates and he may even fall for a false tack (b). Finally you are very close and you may be able to dive through her lee and squeeze up under her lee-bow to finish her off with your back-wind (c).

9.18 Breaking cover ▲

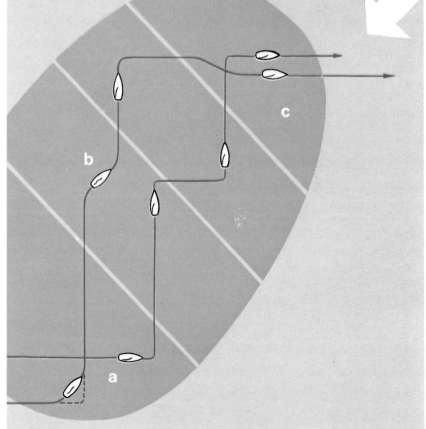

9.19 ▲

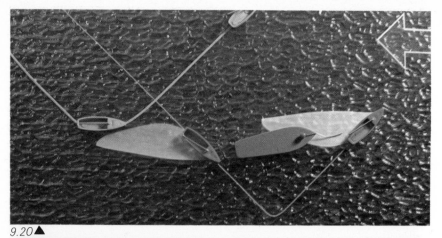

9.20▲

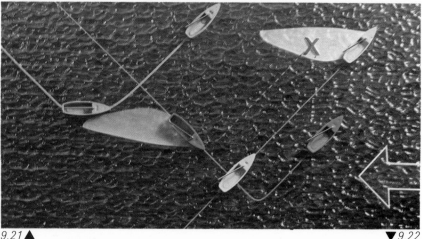

9.21▲   ▼9.22

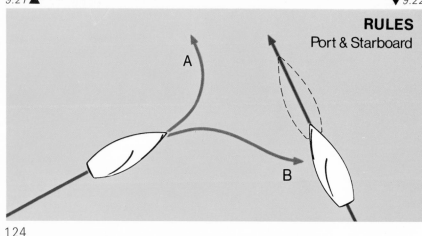

RULES
Port & Starboard

A

B

While doing this don't lose sight of the next mark. It would be too bad to find yourself to windward of the lay-line and that the third boat was now ahead!

The other classic way of breaking cover is to cause an obstruction to intervene. In its simplest form you wait until the covering boat is passing to leeward of an obstruction. and then you tack (*9.20*).

If the obstruction is too far to windward you must make a couple of tacks to get closer. The covering boat will follow on your windward side and you time the tacks to take her just to leeward of it.

On open water courses there are no fixed obstructions such as moored boats but other yachts or even ferries or fishing boats can be used. More usually though you have to make use of other competitors. You time your breakaway so that, if your opponent follows she suffers interference from a third boat (*9.21* and *9.23*).

Port and starboard tacks
When boats converge on opposite tacks the rules say that the boat which is on port tack keeps clear. This is the *Port/Starboard* rule. It is important to realise that the port tack yacht always has two options in avoiding the other boat —to tack herself (*9.22*–A) or to bear away (B). Instinctively the

124

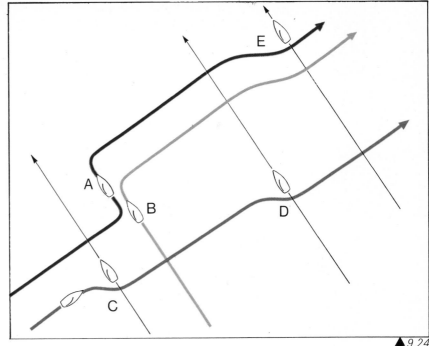

▲9.24

reaction to a sudden hail of 'Starboard!' from a position concealed somewhere behind the headsail is to make a crash-tack, and this is usually the only thing that is possible at such a late stage. Always keep a good lookout to leeward because, apart from a possible collision, it could be nearly as disastrous to one's position to have to tack suddenly to miss a starboard yacht. Equally it is not much use tacking to break cover only to put oneself to leeward of a third boat (9.23). A little forethought and foresight could have avoided the trap.

The helmsman or tactician really does have to keep a mental running plot of the positions of the boats, the marks, the wind and the current. The range of tactics that can be employed on a windward leg is very large and the one to be used at any particular moment depends on the geometrical position of the boats and also the ways in which the strategy of the race can best be carried out.

For example, say that the strategy dictates a long port tack to the starboard side of the course followed by a single tack to the mark. Ideally you start at the starboard end of the line, tack on to port immediately and away you go. But, say this is impossible and you have to make your port tack through a number of starboard tack boats (9.24).

The first point is that you should avoid being forced back on to starboard tack. Fig. 9.24 shows some possibilities and the correct answers, one of which does include a brief period on starboard (A) to force a boat to tack (B). This is a manoeuvre which must be very finely judged and depends on slick crew work, but it can succeed. Remember though that each tack causes a loss of distance. Bearing away gains speed which partly offsets the loss in distance to windward (C, D and E). Furthermore, since you are sailing on port tack presumably there was a good reason for doing so. Therefore, in general it can be said that unless strategy dictates otherwise the preferred tactic when meeting on opposite tacks is to bear away and shoot under the other boat's stern.

125

Tacking on the lee bow

Do I mean that a port tacker should still bear away even when she could almost, but not quite, clear the other boat? Yes—even then it usually pays because by doing so you retain *freedom of action*.

If you tack under the starboard tacker's lee bow (*9.25*) and get it exactly right you can quickly deflect your backwind on to her and force her to drop back and so tack (*9.24*–A). A nice boat-to-boat tactic for a two-boat match race but it is often little more than vindictive to do it in a normal race. As well as losing freedom of action it can so easily go wrong. You lose distance from the tack and there is also a very neat counter to it.

Port has to time her tack exactly right. Too early and she will end up too far away to have any backwind effect. Too late and she risks being disqualified for *tacking too close*. Remember—*tacking* is a 'dead sector' where a boat has no rights and the other boat, in this case Starboard, does not have to *begin* to keep clear until Port is on to her new close-hauled course (*9.26*).

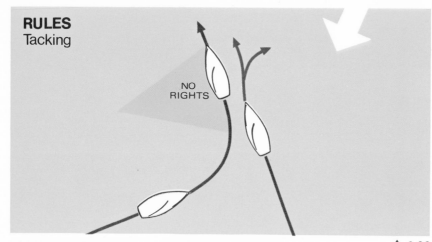

RULES
Tacking

NO
RIGHTS

▲ 9.26

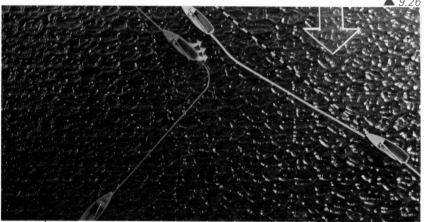

◀ 9.27

Countering a lee bow tack

Put yourself in Starboard's place. How do you protect yourself from a lee bow tack and consequent backwind?

You see a boat approaching and she is not going to be able to cross you. She must either bear away or tack. You immediately start to sail a little free (*9.27*–orange). Be careful that you do it soon enough. If she had already started to bear away she might protest under the rule about restrictions on altering course, by saying that you were preventing her from keeping clear.

You only need to free off slightly, just enough to cause her to miss-time her tack and then, when she is committed, you luff back to close-hauled. She finishes up just too far aft to be able to affect you. The beauty of this type of counter is that the other boat seldom realises that it has happened. It is one of the little tricks that experience teaches and which contributes towards making the expert look so good.

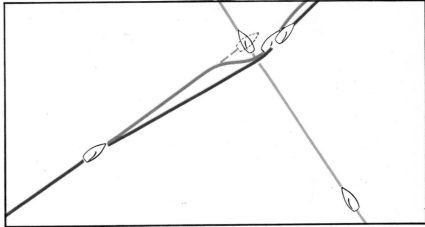

▲ *9.29*

Bearing away for a starboard tack yacht

Now think of Port again; if a good lookout to leeward has been kept, Port can start to bear away early (*9.29*–black). Sudden last minute action is always bad (*9.28*) since the distance sailed is longer, the braking effect of increased rudder action is greater and the correct adjustment of the trim and the sheets is less accurate (*9.29*–red).

There is also the effect on the other boat's helmsman. You want to help him to decide to cross you and then continue on starboard tack. You don't want him to tack close to windward or ahead. If you have already started to bear away (*9.29*–black) he knows that you have seen him and he will not feel he has to make a panic tack at the last moment. If he is obliged to do this he will then certainly protest and you will have difficulty in proving that you were going to keep clear after all.

127

▼9.31

▼9.32

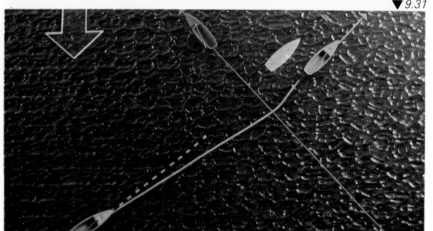

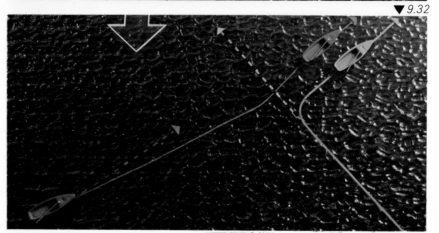

9.30 Unless Port can be sure of crossing it is better to act as in 9.24-A

You want him to feel nice and comfortable and one-up, whereas you know perfectly well, because you have done your planning properly, that he is on the wrong tack and is heading for the less favourable side. So you discourage him from coming with you by making it easier for him to sail on. You bear away slightly good and early and you make sure he knows that you have seen him. You then aim to shave his stern while smoothly luffing back to close-hauled, or even a little higher on account of the lift caused by the other boat's back-wind (*9.31*). He has no chance at all of tacking on top of you. If he does tack his boat will end up on your windward quarter and you will be in the classic lee-bowing position. A very nice piece of work!

There is no real counter to this tactic since it stems from prior superior knowledge on Port's part. However, if Starboard knows this as well then she must tack early, before there is any chance of Port complaining she was prevented from keeping clear (*9.32*). Bearing away slightly to make it more difficult for Port to pass to leeward is unlikely to work in this case but, if Port has obviously not seen you, it is worth leaving your hail of 'Starboard' until pretty late. Too late for her to bear away so that she is forced into a sudden tack to avoid a collision. Then you will certainly end up in complete command of the situation.

Several boats meeting

If there are two or more boats approaching on starboard tack the decision whether to tack or bear away is modified, but do not discount the possibility of bearing off astern of them both rather than tacking. It really is a big disadvantage to tack. However it may be necessary to do so and if so it must be timed exactly right.

The further ahead Port (*9.33–*Orange) is the later she can leave her tack with a better chance of gaining safe leeward position and being able to lee-bow at least one boat. Green may be forced to luff, which could in its turn cause Yellow to tack away followed by Green and then by the Orange boat herself. But Orange thinks that port tack is the most favourable and she now has the other two going that way also. Not the best result!

At all costs Orange must avoid being overrun after her first tack. Green will certainly try to do this by sailing a little free and so Orange must also sail free after her tack to gain maximum speed fast.

If there are two or more overlapping port tack boats an important new rule applies which was touched on earlier and will be discussed more fully shortly. This is the principle that an inside overlapping boat must be given *room to pass an obstruction.*

In a typical example (*9.34*) the leeward port tack boat (Brown) can dictate what will happen. She can,

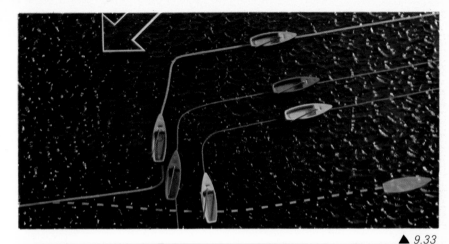

▲ 9.33

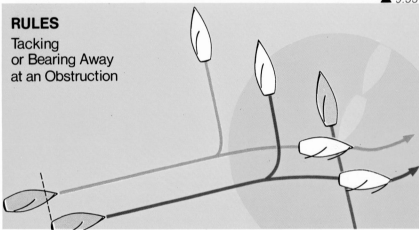

RULES
Tacking
or Bearing Away
at an Obstruction

▲ 9.34

as before, elect to tack to avoid the approaching boat or she can bear away. If she decides to bear away she is obliged to give enough room for Blue to pass to leeward also.

There is a very important limit to this rule which comes into force if they are overlapped when the leading boat reaches a point two lengths from the obstruction, whatever may happen to the overlap thereafter. This limit is commonly known as the *Two-lengths circle* (*9.34*) and, as we shall see, it applies at almost all obstructions or marks which boats may have to pass or round.

Tacking at an obstruction

The other option is for Black to elect to tack but, on open water, she could not do this without infringing the *Tacking too close* rule or the *Port/Starboard* rule. So there is another rule which covers this type of case and also deals with the situation when boats are approaching fixed obstructions such as the shore or shallow water or any object which safe pilotage requires a boat to tack to avoid. This rule, *Tacking at an obstruction*, says that Green (in *9.35*) must hail (usually 'Water, please!'). Red is then obliged to keep clear while Green makes her tack. Red can do this either by electing to tack also or by letting Green know that she will keep clear in some other way (usually by hailing 'You tack!').

Once Green has hailed for 'Water' she starts a chain of reactions which have to be carried out correctly. If Red decides to tack she must do so without delay (b).

Green must then start her tack before Red completes hers (c). Obviously, to avoid backwind after the tack, Green should leave her tack as late as she legally can.

If Red elects to avoid Green in some other way the latter must tack as soon as she hears the reply hail. Red is then obliged to keep clear.

For Red the best tactic depends on the boats' relative positions and the nature of the obstruction. If it is a solid wall or other object Green will usually go close and leave no room for Red to bear away under her stern. But if the boats are tacking against a current up a shelving shore it may be an opportunity for Red to try to get past by bearing away and risking there being enough depth of water to sail a few lengths closer (see the white starboard tack boat in *9.37*). A centreboard boat can raise her board slightly to reduce draught but for a keelboat the risk of being left stranded could be unacceptable. The rewards of a successful manoeuvre are considerable how-

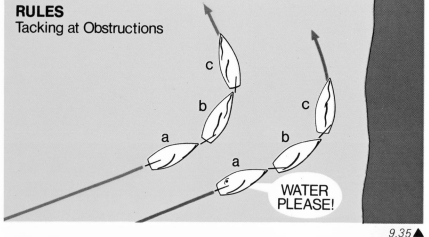

RULES
Tacking at Obstructions

c
b
a
c
b
a
WATER PLEASE!

9.35 ▲

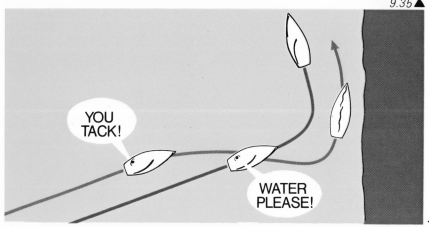

YOU TACK!
WATER PLEASE!

◄ *9.36*

ever, since the new positions of the boats would effectively turn the tables.

There is one exception to this rule—when the obstruction is a mark, which means an object described in the Sailing Instructions as having to be rounded or passed on a particular side. If Red (in *9.35*) could clear the mark without tacking Green is no longer entitled to hail for room to tack. Tactically, this situation would be difficult for Green who ought to have realised that it was about to happen and either bear away and gybe, or bear away to gain enough room to tack.

9.37 Offshore racers tacking close along a shore to avoid a contrary current

The second is usually preferable. The first is the only possible answer if Green is caught napping.

Chapter 10

The Windward Mark

Starboard tack approach

The approach to the windward mark should have been thought about when working out the race strategy. Usually the final approach should be on starboard tack because this gives right of way at a very congested point of the course (*10.1*).

So the first generalisation is to say that if trying to lay the mark on *starboard tack* from some distance away, you should aim to lay it exactly or to over-shoot slightly if rounding to port (the standard Olympic course) (*10.2*).

If approaching on starboard tack to round to starboard you should aim to end up very slightly upwind of the mark so that you are absolutely certain to be as close to it as possible even though another boat might cross you at the last moment and tack on top of you (*10.3*).

It is not easy to lay a mark exactly

◀ *10.1   Approaching on port tack*

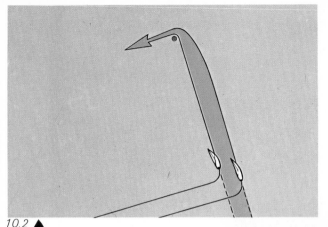

10.2 ▲

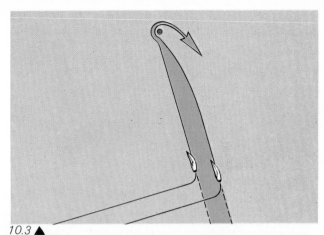

10.3 ▲

from a distance. If there are boats ahead you can often see whether they are going to lay it by sighting along their centrelines as you cross under their sterns (10.4). Remember to allow for leeway. Once you have committed yourself you should find a back-mark to give you a transit bearing. If you have over-shot, the sooner you start to sail free to keep the bearing steady the less distance you will lose on a boat which has laid it exactly.

If you have undershot, make your extra hitch to windward sooner rather than later (10.5). As you approach, other boats will be joining the queue and they will certainly notice that you are not going to lay the mark. They will line up in echelon on your weather quarter until eventually you find you are either unable to tack at all, or you have to tack and bear away under several boats' sterns. You must establish your position on the lay-line in plenty of time.

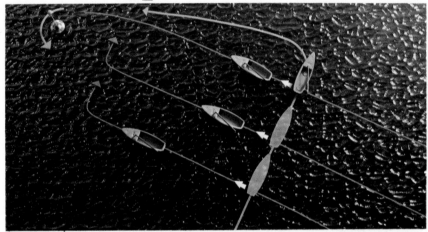

10.4 ▲

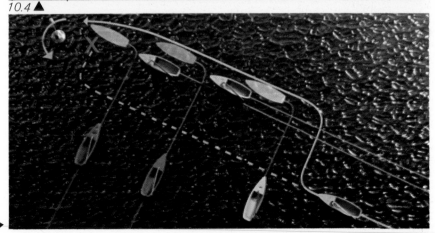

10.5 ▶

▲ 10.6

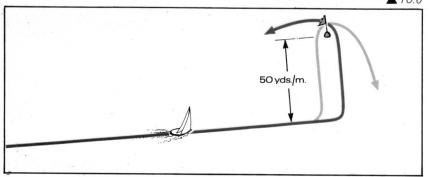

50 yds./m.

▲ 10.7

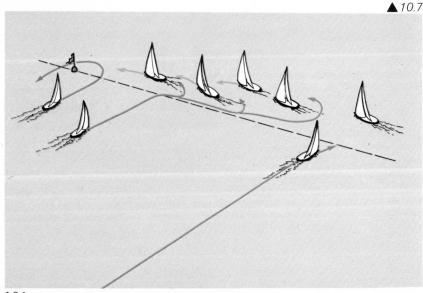

Port tack approach

Approaching from a distance on port tack you should aim to undershoot so that you tack and cover the final fifty yards or so on starboard, even when rounding to starboard (10.7).

Making a final run-in on port tack is extremely risky (see the One-Tonner 'Gumboots' in 10.6) but with luck it could pay big dividends for the following reason. Most boats will be approaching on starboard tack and, because of backwind and general interference they cannot follow closely in each other's wake. Each has to place herself a little to windward of the course of the next ahead to ensure that she does not drop into her backwind and hence fail to lay the mark. Thus each successive boat goes a little too far and has in effect lost a little distance on the leader. The accumulated loss after several boats have got into line can be quite large.

So the temptation to dive into a gap in the line right close to the mark or, if rounding to port, to tack straight round it from a port tack approach, is great and could gain many places (10.8). A bold helmsman can get away with such a manoeuvre pretty often not only because a genuine gap may appear but on account of inaccurate steering by the boats approaching on starboard or by their reluctance to press their rights to the full. But there is no doubt that it is a risky tactic.

◀ 10.8

Right-of-way at the mark

In general the rights-of-way at the windward mark are governed by the *Port/Starboard* rule, the *Windward/Leeward* rule and the other ancillary rules that apply to boats sailing to windward in open water.

Obviously, since boats are sparring for a place in the line of approach, the *Tacking too close* and *Luffing* rules frequently figure in protest incidents and disqualifications.

But there is also a special group of rules in addition which cover all the situations that can occur at *marks and obstructions* and, in some cases, they override the main rules. This group concerns boats which are *overlapping* when the leader reaches the previously mentioned *two-lengths circle*.

The two-lengths circle is a most important limit to remember. It is an imaginary circle round every mark or obstruction with a radius equal to two overall lengths of the boat concerned. When boats *on the same tack* are approaching such a mark or obstruction the main tactical concern of the boat astern is to establish an inside overlap. The main concern of the boat ahead is to prevent an overlap being established (*10.9*).

In practice the ordinary case of whether or not a boat can obtain an inside overlap in time, such as

constantly occurs near gybe marks or other off-wind marks, is unusual at a windward mark. The reason is backwind and wind shadow. It is hard for a boat to overtake another from a position where an inside overlap can be established owing to the wind power being cut off at the critical moment (*10.10*).

Because of this boats approaching a mark from a distance on the same tack fall into a pattern in

which each boat has to place herself slightly to windward of the track of the next ahead. The only overtaking that is normally possible is on the windward side when the boat ahead has misjudged and is having to pinch very close to the wind to weather the mark and is thus moving very slowly. Sometimes one can dive through the lee of a boat that is tacking ahead and this needs instant on-the-spot judgement as to whether (a) one

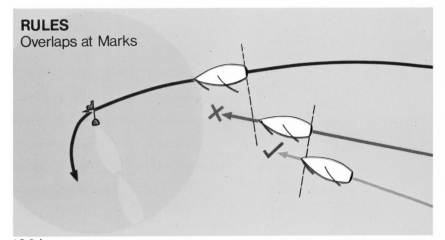

RULES
Overlaps at Marks

10.9 ▲

10.10 ▶

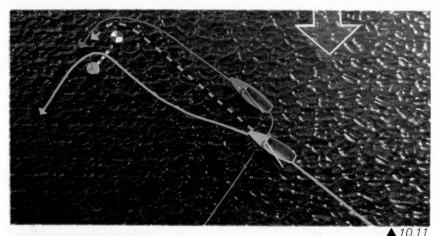

▲10.11

is going to get through the wind shadow and out the other side before the other boat picks up speed, and (b) one does not drop so far to leeward in doing so that the mark cannot be weathered (*10.11*). Note here that an overlap is not established until the tacking boat completes her tack. During her tack she has no rights (see *9.26*).

Tacking into an inside overlap

There is however one other important way an inside overlap can be established and this is by tacking to leeward to obtain right-of-way. There is a special exception to the rule which specifically excludes the usual need to establish an inside overlap before reaching the two-lengths circle in such a case. So that in theory a boat can tack on the lee bow of another right alongside the mark and claim room (*10.12* and *10.13*).

In practice it is not quite so one-sided because the normal *Port/Starboard* and *Tacking too close* rules remain in force which means that, at a critical point in the manoeuvre, the tacking boat has no rights at all (*9.26*). Additionally the moment of establishment of her new right-of-way is not absolutely clear cut and the onus is on *her* to show that she has indeed established this right (*10.16* and *10.12*).

As a tactical manoeuvre it is only likely to work when the tack is

▲10.12   *Tacking into an inside overlap*

RULES
Tacking into
an Inside Overlap

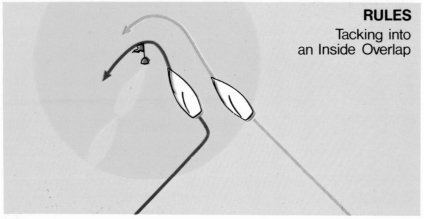

◀*10.13*

made very close to the mark. So close in fact and so smoothly must the tack be made that the boat can if necessary carry its way round the mark. This is on account of the actual behaviour of boats approaching windward marks. They obviously aim to shave the mark as closely as possible but in the last few moments the mark disappears from the helmsman's view behind the headsail and so he is obliged to give a little more room than he strictly needs. Thus, to tack close under a boat's lee bow at a late stage will usually ensure that the mark can in fact be weathered.

● Note the following points:

a) The tack has to be completed, which means that the boat is on the new close-hauled course, before right-of-way is established.

b) The other boat does not have to *begin* to luff clear before this point is established, the onus of proof being on the tacking boat.

● And two further hints:

c) If there is a current in the same direction as the wind or in the sector to windward of the tacking boat—don't try it! It will certainly fail and you will hit the mark (*10.14*).

d) If the current is against the wind or in the sector to leeward of the tacking boat—it would be foolish *not* to try it! You will almost certainly succeed and gain considerably (*10.15*).

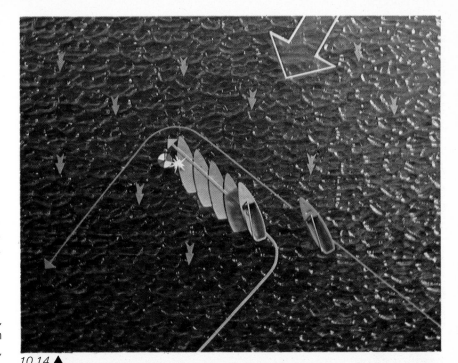

10.14 ▲

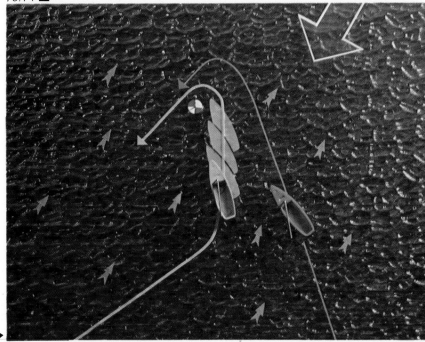

10.15 ▶

Rounding to starboard

The practice today is for big fleets on specially laid courses to round marks to port. The object is to reduce congestion and incidents concerning the rules at the windward mark. A side effect is to cause the long procession of starboard tack boats approaching the mark in echelon and the consequent need for some boats to try the rather risky tactic just discussed. It also tends to prevent boats using the port side of the windward leg in its later stages (*10.17*).

You will certainly be asked to round windward marks to starboard in races which are not of the Olympic type and the tactics are somewhat different (*10.18*). The main object is no longer to be ahead—the all important aim is to be the inside boat (*10.19*) or the boat close *astern* at the mark. This is because a boat cannot tack when close ahead of another for fear of infringing the *tacking too close* rule. Thus if boats approaching on starboard tack are going to tack

10.16 Rubin *crosses ahead of the photographer's boat and tacks into an inside overlap with respect to* Saudade

10.17

10.18

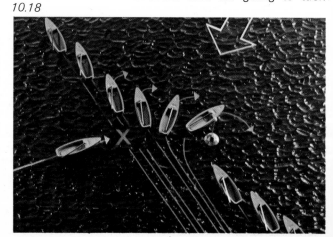

round the mark the one astern holds the advantage. The boat ahead is prevented from tacking until the one astern does so (*10.20*).

There is a trap to watch out for when two boats are in line ahead approaching a mark to tack round it. If they have over-shot and are sailing with sheets slightly eased, which is often the case, the leader will luff close round the mark before tacking. She can go nearly head to wind if she wishes and the other boat then has no option but to go under her stern to leeward and becomes outside boat (*10.21*). But the *tacking too close* rule applies and the outside boat does not have to give enough room for the leader to tack, including the outboard swing of her stern (*10.22*). However, if carried out with care, shooting head to wind first can be a very neat counter manoeuvre for the boat arriving first at the mark.

So, if they are on the same tack, the boat astern must either estab-

10.21 *Before tacking, shoot head to wind to force the boat close astern to pass outside*

10.19

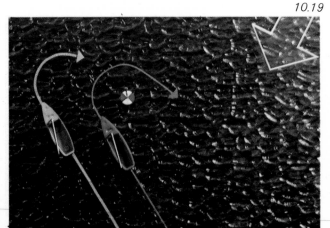

10.20

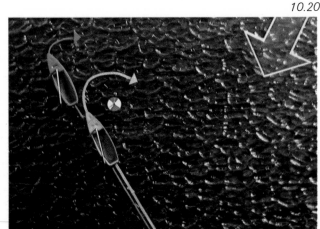

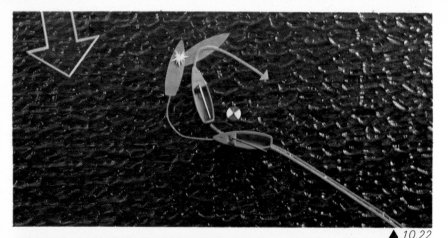

▲ 10.22

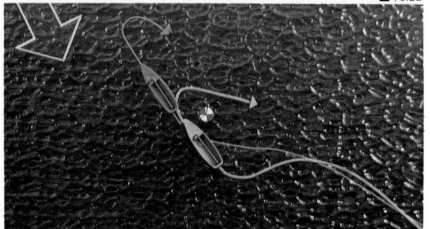

▲ 10.23

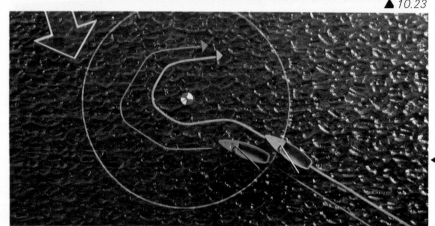

◀ 10.24

lish an inside overlap before reaching the two-length circle or, if she fails to do this, she must slow down by easing sheets or zig-zagging so that she can remain dead astern as they luff round the mark. Since she is then clear astern, the other boat is still bound by the *tacking too close* rule and cannot tack (*10.23*). This is an interesting and important point because, in all other cases when a boat clear astern fails to establish an overlap in time, she has to keep clear of any necessary manoeuvres that the leader may make in rounding the mark, including gybing and avoiding other boats.

Sometimes a tack (or gybe) is an 'integral part of the rounding manoeuvre', which means when it is made close to the mark and the boat does not afterwards spend any significant time on the new tack before finishing the rounding. If so, an outside *overlapping* boat has to give extra room for the tack (or gybe).

Tactically, therefore, the vital point at marks is whether or not an overlap is made *in time* (*10.24*). The rules and possibilities of place changes depend dramatically on this one fact.

11.1 After the windward mark it is ▶ *difficult to change one's plan, once committed*

140

Chapter 11

The Off-Wind Legs

To windward or to leeward?

The general strategy of a reaching leg has to be decided as the windward mark is rounded and often depends on the boat's position in the fleet and whether there are groups of boats close ahead or astern. It may also depend on many other factors such as whether the boat carries a spinnaker or how capable it is of planing and hence, of increasing its speed appreciably relative to the others. Don't forget too that your weather strategy could influence your tactics even on such a comparatively short dash as a reaching leg (*11.1*).

The tendency is for the boats' tracks to bow to windward due to leading boats trying to protect

their· wind supply by luffing. This becomes increasingly difficult as the next mark is approached and they are forced to bear away to reach it, also travelling more slowly on the broader course.

Conversely, a boat which bears away to leeward of the direct course at the beginning can find herself, not only gaining fast at the end of the leg owing to her sailing at a closer, faster angle to the wind, but also she may already have established an inside overlap at the next mark.

On the face of it the second course sounds better but the snag is that she may find herself sailing in the wind shadow of the boats to windward, the effects of which extend some six mast heights down wind. However, the broader initial course may enable a spinnaker to be carried and, if there is a gap astern, she could rapidly establish enough distance to leeward to be clear of the main wind-shadow effect (*11.3*).

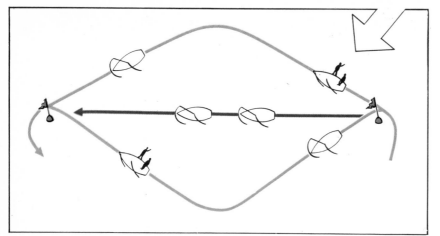

▲ *11.3*

The other main tactic is to go for the windward side by bearing away only enough to gain absolute top boat-speed. This high-speed dash immediately after the mark could take her straight past several boats while they are sorting themselves out and sailing in each others' wave interference. She would end up well to windward of the direct

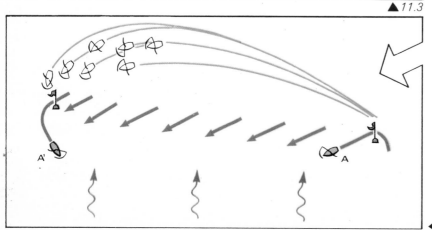

◄ *11.4*

course but this could be compensated for by a smart spinnaker hoist with clear wind and waves to ride on (*11.3*). The course that almost never pays when involved in a group of boats is the middle one but the decision has to be taken early on and then stuck to.

A current on the course will certainly influence this decision. Nine times out of ten, even in top class fleets, you will find that you may be the only crew to remember this and act on it. You could gain a very large number of places on the congested first reach (*11.4*) by going boldly to one side or the other (A–A). In a current the effects of the correct decision become progressively greater at the end of the leg but by then it is too late for the other boats to benefit. This is a frequently successful 'rescue' tactic for a boat which is well down the fleet at the first mark.

Bearing away onto a run

If the next leg is a run, as happens on the second round of an Olympic course, you will bear away around the mark and find yourself meeting boats still sailing to windward (*11.5*). This is a frequent cause of incidents since the running boat is often engaged in hoisting her spinnaker and so she may not be keeping a good look out and her manoeuvring will be restricted as well.

11.5 ▲

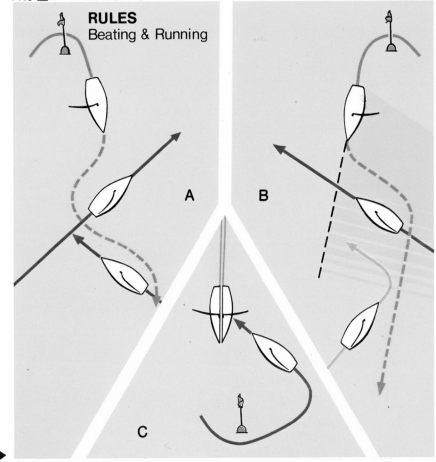

RULES
Beating & Running

A

B

C

11.6 ▶

Remember:

- A running boat on port gybe keeps clear of *all* close-hauled boats (*Port/starboard* rule) even those on port tack (*Windward/ Leeward* rule) (11.6–A).

- A running boat on starboard gybe keeps clear of boats close-hauled on starboard tack which are the ones coming at her from her left (B).

- When nearing the lee mark be prepared to meet close-hauled boats which have rounded the mark and then tacked. If the mark is to be rounded to port they will be on starboard tack and you will have to keep clear (C and 12.12).

Tactically you should always steer to pass astern of a close-hauled boat (11.7). You will lose less distance, whereas if you try to pass ahead you may reach a position where you cannot keep clear at all (11.8).

If you are in the position of being a close-hauled boat in such a situation be careful about *Restrictions on altering course* for a right-of-way boat. If the running boat has altered course to pass under your stern and you then tack you would be wrong if she was thereafter unable to keep clear (11.9–A).

Similarly, if you tack you will have to give time for her to respond and this may legally be longer than

▼ 11.7

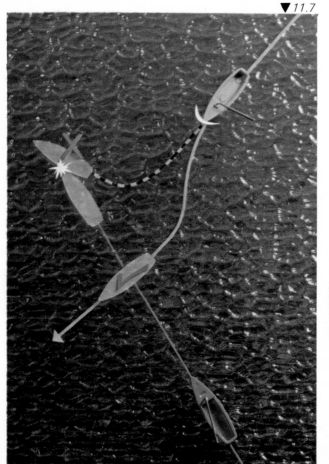

▼ 11.8

you think, especially if she is preparing to hoist or lower her spinnaker (B).

The reaching leg

The question of whether or not two or more boats are overlapped dominates the reaching and running legs in the same way that port or starboard tacks dominates the windward leg. Gaining places on reaching legs involves mainly boat-speed and the necessary boat handling techniques (*11.10*).

The Main rules which are needed are *Luffing, Sailing below a proper course, Windward/Leeward, Clear astern/Clear ahead* and of course *Room at Marks and obstructions*.

The first three act in the same way as we discussed earlier, remembering that this is now a free leg and so a boat cannot bear away from her proper course to hinder a boat to leeward or within three lengths astern which is steering to pass to leeward (*9.10* and *9.11*).

11.10 Boat-speed and overlaps are ▶ *vital on the reaching legs*

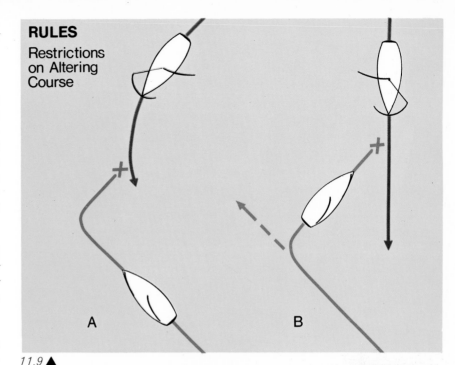

RULES
Restrictions on Altering Course

A   B

11.9 ▲

11.7 & 11.8 Aim to pass astern of a beating boat with right-of-way. Here the running boat will be disqualified.

11.11   A 'continuing obstruction'

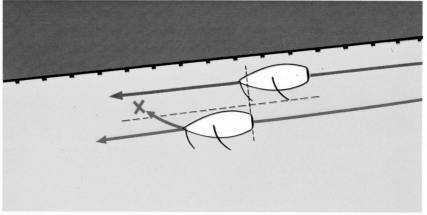

11.13 ▲   ▼ 11.14

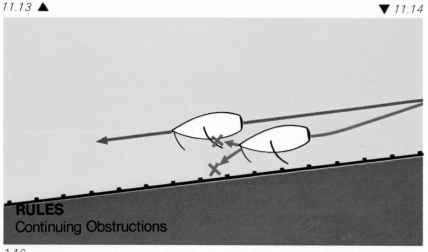

RULES
Continuing Obstructions

Continuing obstructions

The *Marks and obstructions* group of rules however, has some new applications. One of these is the problem of a *continuing obstruction*. This could be a river bank, a shelving shore, shallow water, a line of moorings, a tug towing some barges or even other yachts in the same race. In fact anything that takes a substantial time to pass and which forms an obstruction to free manoeuvring (*11.11*).

The two-length limit distance does not apply to boats approaching a continuing obstruction (*11.12*–A and E), contrary to the case of a mark, and a boat astern can try to establish an inside overlap only if she can do so safely (C and E). The rule says that a boat astern shall only establish an inside overlap if at that time she could pass the boat ahead in safety —which means without hitting the obstruction, running aground or hitting the boat ahead (*11.13*). However once the overlap is established the boat ahead must continue on her course and not luff closer to the obstruction.

There is no doubt that for the overtaking boat it is dangerous to try to pass inside when the obstruction is to leeward (*11.14* and *11.12*–H). Even if she can get right alongside and her boom end is still clear of the obstruction and she has not hit the other boat she still may not be able to get the further room that she may need.

Tactically,   the   boat   astern

should look for a good opportunity to dive in and draw level (*11.12–C*). Sometimes this can be done by making use of a gap in the obstruction or, in the case of a shelving beach, by raising the centreboard part way. The boat ahead can only be as alert as possible and sail as close to the obstruction as she dares.

This rule also applies, for example, to boats running which are trying to pass other running boats which could be in the same race.

Sandwich boat

On a reach or a run it frequently happens that a boat overtakes a group of yachts on the same tack. Can she push her nose in between two yachts and ask for room (*11.15*)? She is overtaking fast and must go somewhere! This is the case of the *sandwich boat*. In general it is dangerous to poke one's bow in between two boats ahead and it is rarely successful if they are determined to keep one out. First, the *overtaking boat keeps clear*, therefore she can have no rights until she has actually established an overlap, and this will only be of help to her if she can do this on the windward boat first.

Second, having established an overlap she cannot sail above her proper course or she would infringe the *luffing* rule. If she is sailing below her proper course, she can ask the windward boat to luff up provided she gives her *room and*

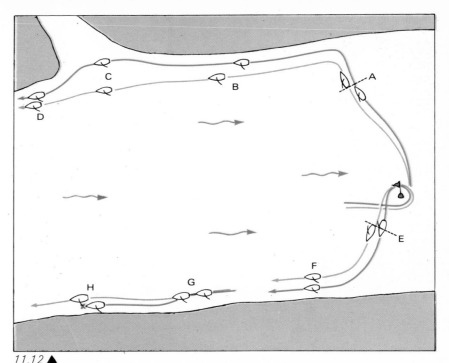

11.12 ▲

11.15 The 'sandwich boat' is asking ▶
for trouble

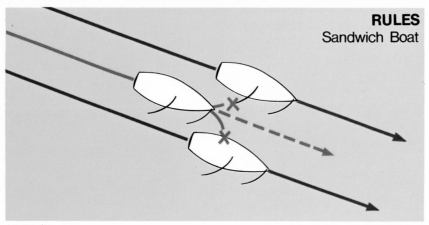

11.16 ▲

Worse than this, the intruder has to keep clear of the boat to leeward as well (*Windward/Leeward* rule) and so if she touches her she is wrong again (*11.16*).

If there are only two boats ahead there is therefore some chance of success, if the windward yacht's stern is overlapped first but very little if the leeward yacht decides to squeeze the overtaker out.

The gybe mark

On approaching a mark, particularly a gybe mark or lee mark, it is vital to obtain an inside overlap on boats nearby so that one can round the mark on the shortest arc and have clear wind thereafter.

The overlap has to be established before the leader of the pair of boats involved reaches the two-length circle. This is a comparatively simple rule to operate if only two boats are involved but frequently there is a group all fighting for position and some may be approaching from quite widely different angles.

There are two main guide lines:

● Start establishing your position with your neighbours well before the circle is reached (*11.18*).
● If you fail to make it you have to keep clear of everyone ahead even when they are gybing, which means going around outside them.

It is not much use to dive in at the last possible moment and ex-

opportunity to keep clear. This may be impossible especially if there are other boats to windward and a mark is being approached. So if she touches the

11.17 Offshore racers gybe round a mark

yacht to windward she would almost certainly fail to prove her case.

In any case, one or both boats would rank as *continuing obstructions* and be limited by the clauses previously mentioned.

pect a group of boats to move over in the last remaining seconds before a tricky gybe. They simply are unable to give you room and the *Limits to overlaps rule* acknowledges this. You could be wrong even though you might have your overlap. Remember the first principles, particularly the need to give boats time to respond to a new situation. So hail your neighbours in plenty of time so that they can respond themselves as well as pass on the need for room to those outside them.

Note what happens to overlaps if boats approach from divergent angles. In these cases too establish your rights by hailing in time for others to respond (*11.19*).

The tactics for the first part of the rounding are to get that vital inside position. For the boat which has tried the leeward course it means sharpening up which will usually increase boat-speed over those to windward (*11.19*–L). She will need this because, as she gets closer she will start to be blanketed and it is essential to secure a position and to hail for 'water for the mark!' as soon as she gets within ear-shot.

If a boat which went for the windward side continues there she will end up rounding outside everyone. At some stage she has to wriggle across to the inside (*11.20*).

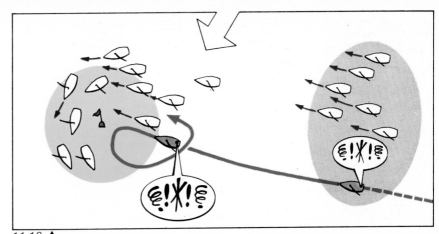

11.18 ▲

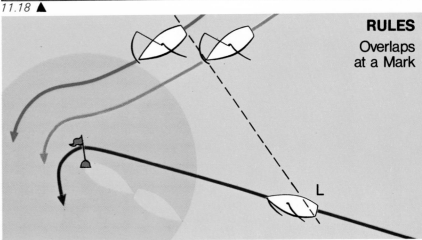

RULES
Overlaps at a Mark

L

11.19 ▲

11.20 ▶

149

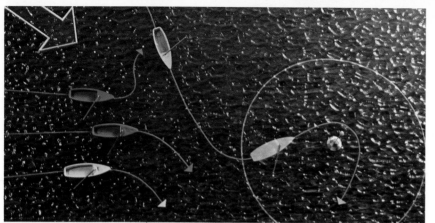

▲ *11.21*

A boat can approach with right of way on starboard tack (*11.21*) but once the two-length circle is reached the *Marks and obstructions* rule takes precedence over all others. Provided she is clear ahead when reaching the circle, all those astern have to keep clear *even when she is gybing* round the mark (*11.22*–A and *11.23*). At all other times a gybing boat has no rights during the gybe.

Another point to note at a mark is that the *Windward/Leeward* rule is also temporarily superseded. Not only can a windward boat claim room (*11.22*–B) but also, if the course to the next mark requires a gybe, a leeward boat *without luffing rights* is obliged to gybe as soon as she has room (*11.22*–C and *11.24*). She cannot sail straight on and invoke the *Windward/Leeward* rule because it is over-ruled by *Marks and obstructions* when the proper course changes at a mark.

So the tactics to be used at a gybe mark are vital. It is easy to win or lose as many as ten places in a big fleet and so start thinking about the gybe as soon as you have rounded the windward mark—or even before!

Luffing the wrong side of a mark

There is a way of breaking an overlap or of stopping an overlap from being established, before a mark is reached but it is not worth trying except in two-boat duels when there is some distance to the

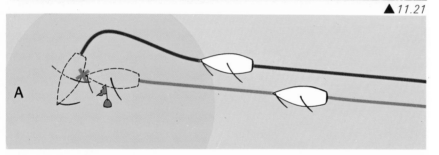

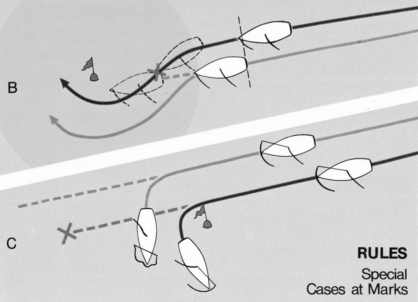

RULES
Special
Cases at Marks

◀ *11.22*

11.23 Keep clear of the boat ahead ▶
when rounding!

next astern, since it is bound to lose some ground.

A boat with luffing rights can luff and take an overlapping boat up to windward of the course to the mark and even sail her on right past it but if she does the latter she has to pass to windward herself before returning (*11.25*). *The Marks and obstructions* rule says that, in this case, the luffing boat must hail ('Luffing!') and also start the luff before reaching the two-lengths circle. In practice it is best to luff hard in the normal way rather sooner than this so that you have enough distance to make a sharp 'S' turn, to break the overlap and get within the circle, before the overlap is re-established.

The exact definition of what is 'to windward of a mark' for the purpose of this rule is a line through the mark at right-angles to the direct course from the last mark. You cannot luff a boat past this line without also going past it yourself.

The second reach

Immediately after the mark the decision again has to be made as to whether to go to windward or to leeward. If you have rounded inside other boats the decision is usually obvious, at least for the first part of the leg (*11.26* and *11.27*–Green). You will find yourself either luffed out to windward

11.24 The course is to the left. The ▶
inside boat must now gybe.

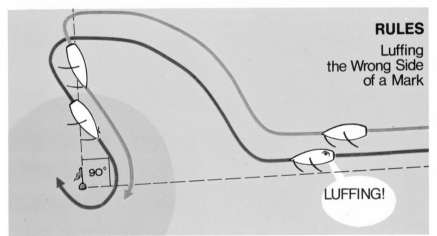

RULES

Luffing the Wrong Side of a Mark

LUFFING!

11.25 ▲

▼ 11.27

by those to leeward and ahead who are desperate to protect their wind supply and to stop you from over-running them, or you will have to do the same to some other boat on your weather quarter. In no time at all there will be wide separation between the luffing boats to windward and those taking the opposite course of bearing off to leeward far enough to get clear air (Red).

But it may be essential to cross to one side or the other soon. Get a transit bearing on some fixed point behind the next mark and see if you are keeping it steady. Is there a current pushing you one way or the other? Poor steering can lose many places on this type of reach and the effects rapidly worsen as the next mark is approached.

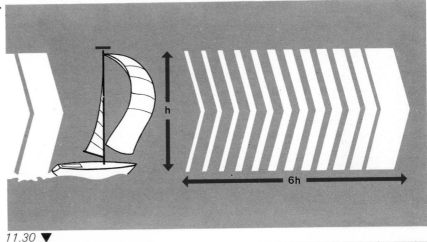

11.29 ▶

Blanketing

The effects of wind-shadow (11.28) can be felt as far as six mast heights away but obviously at the greater distances it is relatively weak and the disturbed strip is narrow (11.29).

On any course, if you want to throw disturbed wind on to another boat, it is the apparent wind which matters. Thus you only have to sail so that your mast-head flag is pointing directly at, or slightly astern of, another boat for you to be certain that she is receiving the most disturbed wind that is possible (11.30). This technique is effective in pulling back a running boat and also in preventing a reaching boat from passing to leeward.

11.30 ▼

153

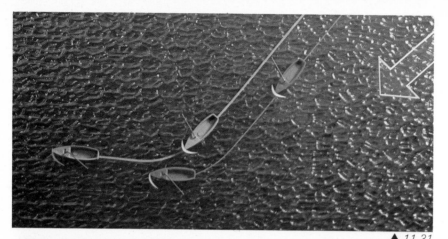

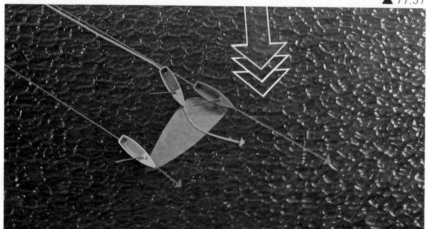

▲ 11.31

▲ 11.32

If you are a running boat and want to break cover the only answer is to gybe neatly and smoothly away and hope you can take the attacker by surprise so that she fails to follow you fast enough (11.31).

To break through wind-shadow on a reach is sometimes easiest, especially for planing dinghies, very close to the covering yacht. This may seem strange since the blanketing zone is widest and most intense there but there are special reasons why it can work especially if the crew's reactions can be well co-ordinated and very quick (11.32).

First, the zone is here sharp-edged but, on the leading side the wind-speed is increased and angled slightly more from ahead. Second, the wave system of the boat ahead is such that if you bear away and accelerate on a puff the boat can break through the lee quarter wave, then ride on its face through most of the dead patch, reaching the new and increased wind on the other side at the correct angle to take advantage of it.

Further down the disturbed zone it is very difficult to tell exactly where the edge is, there is no wave system to help and no increased wind on the other side. So either make your attempt from very close or go right to the extreme outer tip (11.32).

◄ 11.33 Nice wave conditions for a successful break-through but the boat needs to be on a closer reach than this.

A stern chase

Often the race becomes a procession in its later stages and the
problem for a second boat is how
to close the gap on the leader and
get within striking distance
(11.34). In these conditions the
leader will be closely watching the
boats astern and will certainly be
preoccupied with covering. Here is
your chance to increase his ner-
vousness and anxiety and cause
him to make mistakes. It is really a
very simple technique but it is surprising how successful it can be
(11.35).

You wait for a slight increase in
wind and then luff smoothly a
small amount (A). Not so much
that he is bound to notice im-
imediately, but just enough to take
you gradually and at slightly increased speed to windward of his
course.

Eventually he will suddenly
realise that you are up on his
weather and he will alter course to
cover (B), whereupon you bear
away also very smoothly (C).

The closer you get the more
anxious he becomes and the more
effective is the technique. Each
time that he makes his alteration it
is a little sharper than yours (D)
and he is putting on the brakes.
You should close the gap substantially though you may have to
wait until the mark or the next leg
before attempting to pass (E).

11.35 ▼

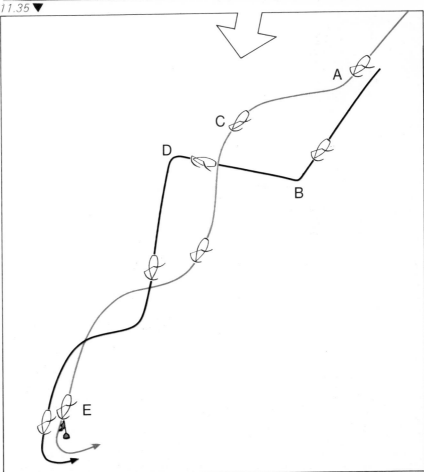

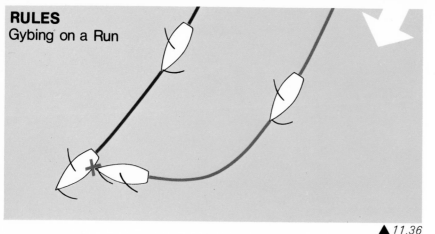

RULES
Gybing on a Run

▲ 11.36

Gybing on a run

The *tacking and gybing* rule covers the case of gybing too close in the same way as for tacking too close. A boat has no rights during the gybe but this is a very much shorter manoeuvre than a tack. However, especially in heavy weather, your boat may be only partially under control immediately after the gybe and it would be your fault if an incident occurred before another boat had a chance of getting clear. You cannot gybe on to starboard tack and then luff into a port tack boat without giving her ample time to gybe herself and keep clear (*11.36*).

An interesting point is that a gybe breaks an overlap and can establish a new overlap situation. Hence, luffing rights previously lost by dropping behind the mast abeam position can be re-established without drawing clear ahead or astern or more than two lengths abeam by doing two quick gybes.

One more point—boats out of control or capsized have to be avoided at all times. They rank as *obstructions* (*11.37*). If you are yourself out of control and it is not obvious, you should hail any approaching boats.

◀ *11.37   The rules say you must avoid boats out of control!*

Chapter 12

The Lee Mark and After

12.1   470s approach a mark

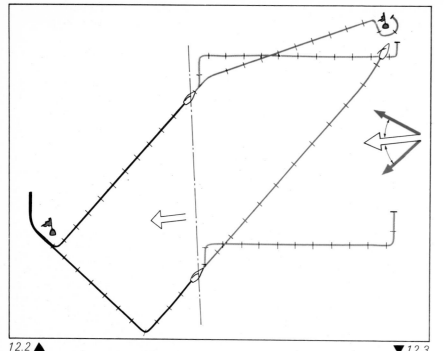

12.2 ▲ ▼12.3

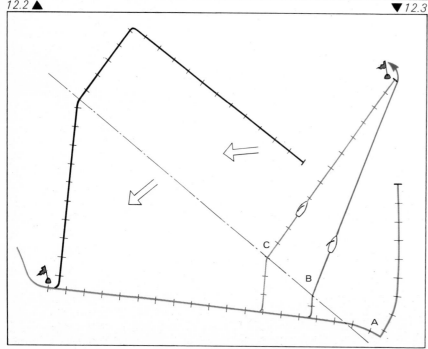

Picking the best tack

Approaching the lee mark (*12.1*) the problem is not only how to establish an inside overlap or, if ahead, how to prevent one being established, but what to do after the mark is rounded. The exact wind direction has a bearing upon this. Has it shifted since the last windward leg? Is it still shifting rhythmically and, if so, which side will be favoured?

The normal the rule is to sail first on the tack which takes you nearest to the next mark. The theory behind this is that, if the wind subsequently frees (*12.2–*Green) on that tack it is potentially bad with respect to your position versus other boats but you will have minimised problems by getting as near the mark as possible. If the wind heads (Red) you simply tack in the ordinary way and you should always be nearest the mark.

Of course, if you *know* how the wind will shift you can plan a much more accurate course to take utmost advantage from it and we have discussed this possibility in Chapter 5. For example, the seabreeze may be shifting with the sun and will go on shifting in the same general direction. The starboard tack may already be the longest but it will still pay to go to the starboard side of the course as soon as possible to pick up the next veering shift (*12.3*–A). Remember it will reach that side first but also the boats that have overshot slightly will be able to free off and go faster. So it will pay to go a little farther (B) than the theoretically shortest track (C). The rule is:

● Sail towards the expected shift.

If you had not done your homework and so have nothing on which to base a decision you should take the long tack first because the odds are that the wind will head back to a more nearly true beat.

Unfortunately, it is not usually possible to assess the true wind direction when reaching owing to the variations in boat-speed and its resulting effects on apparent wind though, on an Olympic course or similar triangle, some idea can be gleaned from the relative closeness of the two reaches, i.e. if the second reach is closer than the first then the starboard tack will be the longer one but remember to take current into account. Knowing this fact will at least be some help and *may* be significant if very different from the wind direction experienced on the first windward leg.

On a run it is quite easy to use the compass and the masthead indicator to get true wind and even to note rhythmic shifts. They can be compared directly with the information previously put on to the note-board.

12.4   Your position at the start of the next windward leg depends on the correct approach to the mark

The approach

The strategy for the windward leg influences the approach to the mark (*12.4*). Obviously an overlap on a boat ahead means that this boat is as good as beaten but it also means that unless you can get far enough ahead of her after the rounding to put her in your windshadow she will interfere with your strategy. She may even lee-bow you and force you to tack away. Nothing is worse at this point to find oneself trying to pinch out of the backwind of a boat which is herself pinching (*12.5*–Orange). You lose speed and, if you have to tack, are dead in the water at a point where waves are lumpy and confused and the wind is cut up by other boats.

So the question is whether to go for a smooth, fast rounding and to sail free and fast on the same tack to get clear (Green), or to get close to the mark at all costs so that one can tack almost immediately (Blue).

The fastest course to the mark is an approach from leeward (*12.6*–Orange). Boats which have taken the windward option on the reaching leg find themselves having to protect their weather as they near the mark by luffing to windward of the direct course and end up sailing slowly with the wind almost dead aft (Green and Yellow). On the other hand, though the leeward option allows a boat to luff and accelerate just before rounding,

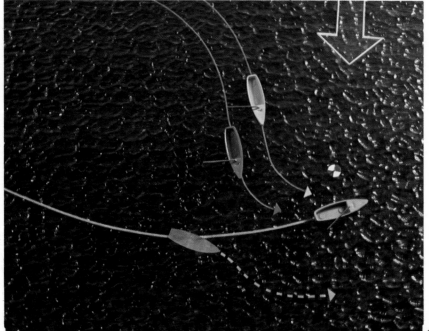

◀ 12.6

she may find herself blanketed by those to windward at a critical moment and, of course, she has to give room to those with overlaps (dotted track). This could mean that she starts the next leg a length or more to leeward which can be a serious loss at this point.

There is a good deal of scope for opportunism here. If a group of boats are fighting for overlaps to windward then a fast dash from the lee side might take them all (*12.7–A*). In any event they will be moving slowly after a broader approach and a consequent too-sharp rounding and so a leeward boat might shoot through their lee just after the mark even if she rounds astern of them.

If the windward queue is more straggly it may be possible for a leeward boat to cross boldly just before the mark and establish a position in a gap in the line (B).

On the other hand a boat to windward may be able to gybe on to starboard tack and so have right of way over everyone but she should remember to hail in plenty of time or her rights may do her no good (*12.8*)! She should also remember that, even though she is on starboard tack she still has to keep clear of boats rounding ahead which have reached the two-lengths circle before her because the *Marks and Obstructions* group of rules overrides the *Port/Starboard* rule here.

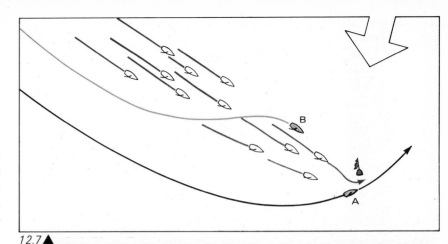

12.7 ▲

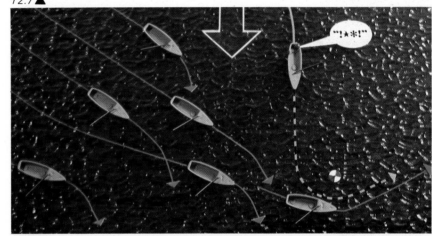

12.8 ▲

12.9 ▶

12.12   *Half-Ton Cup racing*

Another place-winner is to profit from a poor rounding by squeezing in between the boat ahead and the mark but this is comparatively dangerous because the attacking boat has no rights at all and ends up as windward boat too. It works most often when there is a lee-going current and in fact it would be foolish not to try it in such a case (*12.9*).

Look out for the extreme cases which also need bold action. One such is a fleet running with a current and going to round a lee mark (*12.10*). It often pays to slow down and arrive astern of a group and thus round close to the mark and end up in control on their windward side (*12.11*).

Another is rather similar when very light winds are causing a nearly stationary bunch to collect at a mark or obstruction (*12.10*). Keep speed up and sail right round outside the bunch.

Covering

After the mark there are two distinct disadvantages to tacking immediately (*12.12*). One is that distance is lost in making the tack and the second is that it takes one dead to leeward or even straight amongst, boats which are still approaching. Even though the beating boat may have right of way if she is on starboard tack she has to sail through disturbed air and concentration may suffer.

▼ 12.11

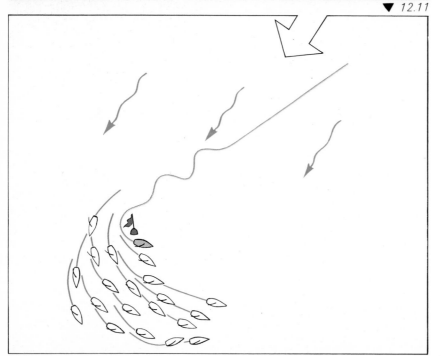

For this reason it may not pay to tack to cover an opponent who tacks immediately. It may be better to stay on for a while to ensure clear wind (*12.13*). It depends how important the duel is and how many other boats are within striking distance. It happened just like this in a vital race in the One-Ton Cup when our principal rival for the championship tacked immediately after the lee mark and passed astern of us. It was a hard decision to take to keep going when all the crew

12.13 ▼

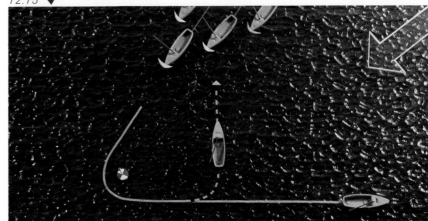

knew that one of the 'Golden Rules' of racing was to cover the boat next astern.

The classic covering manoeuvre at a lee mark is to tack immediately and then tack back before your opponent has reached the mark (*12.14*). You are then dead to windward and in complete control whatever she may do. The one fatal mistake is to follow the dotted track and find yourself just tacking back as she rounds the mark. She can then break away and you will be dead in the water.

More usually you will not have enough lead to do this and will have to follow when your opponent tacks. She then has a measure of control as was discussed earlier (*12.15*).

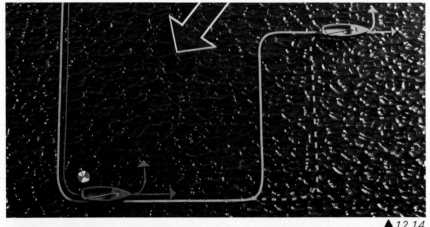
▲*12.14*

◀*12.15*

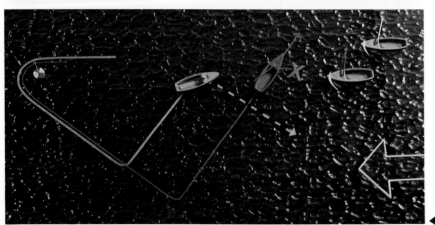
◀*12.18*

12.19 ▶

Breaking cover

Soon after rounding a lee mark (*12.16*) is the best time to try to break away from close cover (*12.17*). The surest technique is to tack immediately after the mark (*12.18*–Orange) whereupon your opponent will cover and you can then 'wipe her off' on one of the approaching boats which are still running. In other words you tack back when the covering boat is unable to follow owing to there being another boat in her way.

The other method is to tack in a position where she cannot follow without being herself covered by another boat. Orange tacks, Green follows and finds herself covered by Yellow (*12.19*).

Sometimes a false tack can work but this is a battle of wits between the two helmsmen and depends for its success on how closely they are watching each other (*12.20*). In your efforts to get clear wind and to break free do not forget the

boats astern who will be watching closely for an opportunity to pass both of you.

▼*12.20*

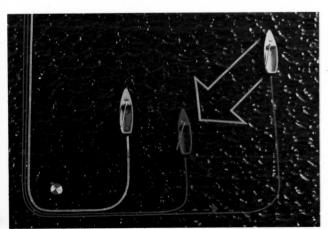

165

Chapter 13

The Finish

Whether the finish is at the end of a windward leg, as is most common in championship racing, or on any other point of sailing (*13.1*) the most useful thing to know about the line is which end is nearest. Obvious, you may say, but surprisingly often neglected!

The Sailing Instructions may state where the line will lie and you can plot it on a chart but, more usually, you are faced with a committee boat and a mark in the distance but no way of telling how the line between them is angled. The golden rule is:

● Keep between your opponent and the next mark.

It becomes more tricky to follow the nearer you approach since you do not know which *is* the next mark (i.e. the nearest end) (*13.2*)! The best advice is to keep your options open until as late as possible and so plan the approach to the line with this in mind.

13.1   A close finish!

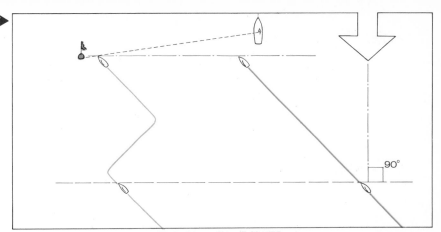

There are two certain race-losers at the finish. One is to be blanketed by the Committee boat as you pass astern of it (*13.3*–Green). The other is to be unable to tack for the line owing to a boat on your windward quarter (Yellow). Avoid these traps by thinking ahead.

If the committee boat is at the starboard end you can still cross at this end by means of a final approach on port tack which is not usually dangerous since there are fewer boats to look out for. If it is essential to approach from outside the committee boat, lay a course slightly to windward of its stern (*13.4*–Orange) and then bear away to pass as quickly as possible through its wind-shadow close to its stern. You will also be able to claim room from overlapping boats to leeward and should be able to shake off a boat close astern also (Green).

If there is a boat on your windward quarter you must open up a gap so that you can tack by sailing free and fast (*13.6*–Orange). Then you may be able to cross close ahead or perhaps dive under Green's stern and shoot head to wind. A covering boat is in a very strong position here. By accurate tacking and careful steering she can make it almost impossible for the covered boat to break away since the manoeuvring space becomes more restricted the closer the line is approached.

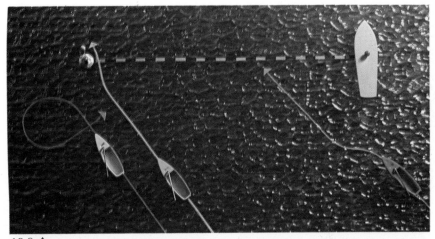

13.3 ▲

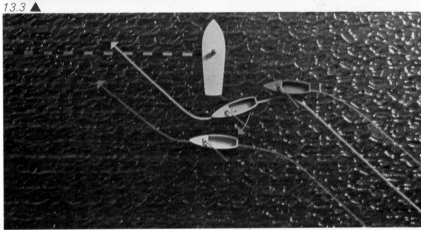

13.5 *The far Soling wins by diving under the stern of the centre boat. The nearest boat has to tack and may not be able to squeeze round the end mark*

Make sure that you know the exact definition of the line. It is often different from the starting line, especially if the latter was a transit. Finishing lines are usually between two marks, one of which is the committee boat—but which part of the committee boat? Make sure you know. A luff at the critical moment could gain you the extra two feet you need to beat the boat to windward (13.5). But you have to know where the line is to be able to judge it accurately.

The race ends when the leading part of a boat first cuts the line but remember that the rules still apply until you have *cleared* the line (13.7). In 13.8 the boat may be allowed to re-round the mark if the sailing instructions say so but would not finish until she cut the line a second time. I once watched a Danish crew at the end of a long and gruelling final race in a world championship in almost a flat calm. They made a roll-tack to cross the line and then capsized before they were clear and drifted on the current into the mark. They lost the title!

▲ 13.6

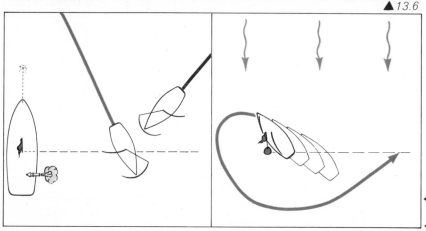

◀ 13.7 (far left)

◀ 13.8

Chapter 14

Problems and Protests

Problems

Until quite recently if you broke any of the racing rules, however minor, it was a case of 'sudden death' and you were disqualified from a placing in that race. If you knew that the fault was yours you were obliged to retire from the race immediately.

The standard of observance of the rules varies from place to place and class to class. Usually, minor accidental infringements are overlooked but touching a mark—never. However, under the greater pressures of the more highly developed racing of today where there is so much more at stake for some of the competitors, the rules were starting to be neglected or even blatantly ignored. In an effort to improve the situation the IYRU introduced alternative penalties for some rules which enabled a boat to continue in the race but with some loss in position or points.

The only alternative which is included in the rules themselves is *re-rounding a mark* if you touch it, but even this can be countermanded by a sailing committee. Of the others some are in the Appendices whilst still others are special rules made for specific purposes such as the time penalty for Offshore Racing boats who are over the line before the starting signal of a long race.

These alternatives are penalties for acknowledging a wrong-doing and include making two 360° degree turns immediately after the incident, or accepting a 20 per cent drop in placing for that race. There are difficulties with both of these ideas and they are not yet in very general use. So, apart from re-rounding a mark you will normally have to expect 'sudden death' for breaking rules.

The reason for such severe penalties lies in the imprecision of sailing. Unlike a road accident where the damaged cars can remain where they are until police have assessed the position, yachts drift apart or sail on leaving only hazy memories of a swiftly changing situation in the minds of the crews. The severity of the penalty was intended to cause sailors to take more care and avoid incidents happening, though the realities of racing small boats in the huge fleets of today have caused a partial breakdown and hence the efforts to make improvements.

Protests

If an incident cannot be solved on the race course, or if a third party witnesses rule breaking, one or more boats may find themselves *Protested*. This is the formal method, that is precisely laid down in the rules, for investigating an incident and resolving who is at fault. The penalty is usually disqualification and sometimes there is the extra penalty of a greater loss of points for an incident which has to go to protest compared with one which is solved on the water.

Protests are also used as evidence for insurance companies (or

169

even courts) to decide on insurance claims between boats for the cost of repairing damage or loss.

A protest is usually heard immediately after the race by a committee of about three independent people specially appointed by the Sailing Committee. The result of a Protest will affect the race results and so it must be solved quickly especially if the race is one of a points series. Sometimes therefore the usual right to appeal to the National Authority is specifically denied.

Protests are very common and crews should not feel frightened or in any way ashamed of being involved in one in spite of perhaps a rather heated exchange of opinions at the time of the incident. Everyone knows that memories can play tricks and that the exact positions of the boats at the time are nearly impossible to fix accurately afterwards. The protest committee should include people who are not only experienced in interpreting the rules but who are themselves active in racing and who can thus patiently find out, by referring to their own experience, what actually happened.

How a protest works

The routine is strictly laid down in the rules and can be summarised for the protestor as follows:

● After an incident, if you are sure you were right and that the other boat has affected you or your placing, you should hoist a *protest flag (3.11)* in the rigging. Flag B, which is a red swallowtail, is the universally accepted signal and you should have one on board. The committee will not hear the protest unless the finishing boat has recorded that a flag has been flown, or unless the facts only become clear later.

● Tell the other boat as soon as possible that you are protesting, unless she retires.

● Find witnesses to back up your case. Remember that if the onus is on you to prove that you had established right-of-way in time (after a tack, for example) you will definitely need some outside evidence of this. It would be a waste of time protesting without it and you will almost certainly lose *even though in reality you may have been right*.

● Write out the details of the protest including a small sketch plan of the positions of the boats and the rule which you think was broken. If you have incorrectly assessed the situation or have written down the wrong rule it does not affect the protest or prejudice your case (*14.1*).

● Inform the sailing committee, hand in the written protest and pay any deposit money, which is returned afterwards unless the protest is considered to be frivolous.

● Collect your witnesses together at the appointed place and time. If you are not there the protest will be dismissed or may go against you by default.

The hearing

● The protestor and protestee are called in alone. The facts of the incident are established by asking the protestor to position model boats on the table and then the protestee does the same. There will usually be differences in positioning which will often be the critical thing for the committee to establish before they can apply the right rule and decide the protest.

● With the two principals present, witnesses are called one by one to give their versions and are questioned by the principals and by the committee.
The committee can call for any other help they may need and when they think they have all the facts they ask everyone to leave while they talk it over.

● The committee then call in the two principals and deliver their verdict. They say that they will give it in writing if required and that there is a right of appeal against their interpretation of the rules, but not on matters of fact. They then hand back the deposit money and deliver the written verdict to the Sailing Committee.

When to protest

If there is a collision, a boat should either retire or protest. Legally there is no other option. Frequently no-one retires and no-one protests. Since most incidents are very minor and no-one's position is affected this might seem to be sensible but it unfortunately leads to mass non-observance of the rules which hurts everyone in the end.

Protests are tedious and take valuable time just when the committee is particularly busy working out results and when crews are changing clothes and packing up boats to go home. No-one wants them and even committees have been known to obstruct crews from putting in genuine protests. But it is important to remember that a third boat witnessing two boats touching may protest afterwards if no-one has retired. There is a let-out in the rules which enables the committee to dismiss the protest if minor contact was unavoidable but this rule has had the effect of forcing crews to put in protests even though common sense would indicate that the incident be ignored.

Tactically therefore, if there is contact between boats you should protest because otherwise 'big brother', in the shape of another boat or the committee, may have seen the incident and you could then find yourself at a protest hearing without adequate preparation and with the committee perhaps somewhat prejudiced against you.

However it is nearly always unwise to put in a protest unless it is unavoidable. Apart from the psychological strain of having to spend valuable time gathering evidence, preparing a case and

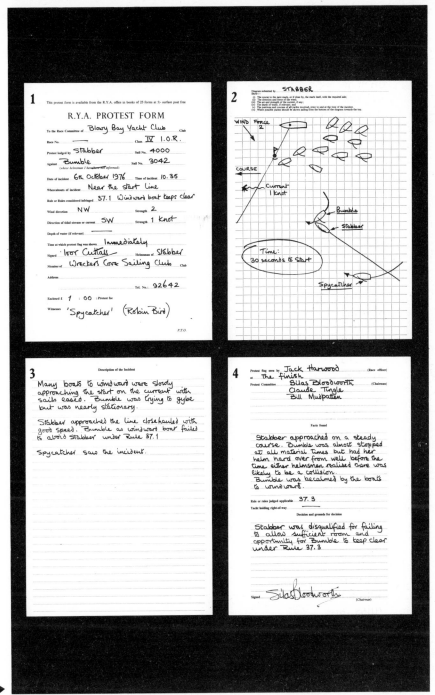

14.1   A filled-in protest form ▶

then fighting it in committee there is the not unlikely event that you might well lose!

It frequently happens that an apparently watertight case is broken open by the chance remark of a witness which totally changes the rules which apply. The application of the rules in borderline cases, especially where there is a change-over from one boat having right-of-way to another, is so fine that the result could easily swing one way or the other and depends on the committee forming a firm opinion of the facts from out of a jumble of conflicting stories.

The moral is to cultivate in yourself and your competition a spirit of give-and-take which, at the same time does not ignore the rules. It is a delicate balance which must be based on a desire to win fairly and a sound knowledge of basic rules and tactics.

Tactics for the protester

Assume, however, that an incident has occurred. One skipper decides to protest and, of course, he will want to make the most of the situation and gain maximum advantage.

There is nothing to stop a protester attempting to win by falsifying the facts as well as indulging in a psychological battle designed to smear or confuse the other crew but the first would be illegal and the second would, I suggest, be quite contrary to the spirit of a great sport like sailing.

However, there is no doubt that a certain amount of 'gamesmanship' can be used to maximise ones chances or minimise the risks, without saying anything untrue. The dividing line between being scrupulously fair and misleadingly dishonest is vague and who is to say where it might lie? I can only suggest certain courses which I hope would be acceptable to the majority.

The first thing to get clear is that there should be no possibility of a protest being vicious or vindictive. It would be quite unfair and against the spirit of the sport for a protest to result from anything except a genuine mistake or misjudgement. This is not to say that it is wrong to use the rules in a tactical way. The failure of the other crew to respond to a tactical manoeuvre would be a justifiable ground for protest whether they had fully realised the implications of the manoeuvre or not. But once the incident has occurred the protester can take certain immediate steps to swing public opinion his way and to demoralize his opponent.

This is the most important moment of the race for a protester and the positions of the boats must be indelibly implanted in the minds of everyone within range. Therefore shout loudly (and perhaps even angrily) to draw attention to the incident and pointedly hoist a protest flag. Call to nearby crews to note where the boats lie and ask them to be witnesses later. They

can hardly refuse and so note their numbers down and then, while everyone, and not least the victim, is somewhat shaken by your forceful behaviour, just quietly sail off and get on with your race.

You should be several points up already and you will have fulfilled the rule obligation to inform the other boat too. On crossing the line make sure the committee know you have a protest and against whom.

On getting ashore be quiet, cool and efficient. Write out the protest, hand it in, find out the time of the hearing and then go and collect your witnesses. It goes without saying that a protester must be sure of his facts and so, when talking to witnesses only ask those to be present who see it your way and are going to be reliable and definite in their evidence. A poor witness is worse than useless. Don't forget knowledgeable observers, particularly members of the Sailing Committee, who may have seen the incident. They can be most valuable with their impartial and semi-official status and will carry great weight.

Before the hearing, prepare your case thoroughly and know the rules involved. When you come to give evidence give it clearly, briefly and authoritatively. Place the model boats in position accurately first time. Give the impression that you know exactly what you are doing.

Your tactic is to dispute every-

14.2   '... the positions of the boats must be indelibly implanted in the minds of everyone within range'

thing that your opponent or his witnesses say but don't break in — always speak with the chairman's permission. Try to get them to contradict each other and if they do so, gently but firmly point out this discrepancy. Try to show that the witness could not possibly have seen the incident properly or that his judgement of an overlap, for example, was obscured or unreliable owing to an oblique viewpoint. Ask him what the relevant rule is. He will often get it wrong and look foolish.

Bear in mind that you are trying to impress the jury with your superior knowledge and your genuine feeling of injury. It is also a help to look clean and tidy when

you appear. In fact, put yourself in the position of the jury who want to establish the facts clearly and make a decision. Help them all you can.

Tactics for the protestee

To have a protest put in against you is inevitably going to be worrying and upsetting psychologically but, with care it can often be turned to advantage and frequently the protester may find himself as the culprit. Fortunately for you, the rules are very imperfectly understood, even by race committees, and the results are far from obvious even to comparative experts.

As with the protester, the first

and most immediate need is to speak to other boats nearby to give their crews a reference point so that their memories can focus on the relative positions of the boats at the time. You must take down their numbers on your note pad and it is an advantage also to put up a protest flag even if you cannot immediately work out what your case will be.

Try to work up a bit of hate and a sense of injustice against your opponent which will increase your adrenalin and enable you to get on with the race and make up for lost time. Do not think any more about the incident until after the finish but then you have to start the hard work!

Inform the committee of your protest and then try to speak to all the witnesses you can find as you are sailing home and as soon as you get ashore. Draw out a sketch plan of what happened and try to work out how it can be turned to your advantage.

The main thing is to get into an attacking mood. Don't feel that what you did was wrong—however blatant a foul it may have seemed. Even an apparent clear cut Port and Starboard incident may have been influenced by other boats or obstructions. A very useful line of attack is to use the rule limiting the *right-of-way yacht altering course*. If you can show that he has balked you in your efforts to keep clear or has misled you by his actions you are half way to reversing his claims or at least getting the protest dismissed.

The same principle applies to the protestee as to the protestor at the hearing. Be clean, tidy and helpful and state your case briefly and clearly. Be completely definite about your statements and views, which presupposes that you have worked out your plan of action beforehand. You must know the rules you are going to invoke and how they apply.

You will be unlucky if you meet a really competent protester. If your man is talkative, indefinite or confused in any way — play on that and try to increase the confusion. With a little luck the jury will at least throw the protest out.

I hope that this book will have given you an insight into the rules of the game and the way they are applied. Tactics are the product of rules. Use them to have fun—and win!

Appendix: Racing Rules Index

The international authority is the International Yacht Racing Union (IYRU) whose address is 60 Knightsbridge, London SW1, England.

The IYRU issues the official Rule Book, which is amended at the end of each Olympiad (4-year period ending in a leap-year). The IYRU also controls all aspects of racing, except some specialised branches which are self-administered, and acts through National Authorities in most countries.

The Racing Rules cover all aspects of the conduct of a race, but it is mainly the section concerning rights-of-way for boats when racing which concerns us here. This is Part IV, rules 31 to 46. Protest procedure has a section to itself—rules 68 to 78.

Official Rule Books can be obtained from your own National Authority or from the IYRU. There are some other publications which contain all or part of the official rules text, but since they have to be updated every four years, only a few are completely reliable in this respect (see Bibliography).

The following is a cross-index between the text of this book and the IYRU Rules.

Main references are in bolder type. Illustration references are in italic.

Text references:	Page:	Rule:	Official title:
Fair sailing	9, **24**, 99	**Introduction**	Fair sailing
Unfair propulsion Means of propulsion	**24**, 85, (6.28), 110, (8.11)	**60**	Means of propulsion
Time to respond Room and opportunity	**24**, 133, (8.20), 127, 144, 147/8, 149, 156		(Implied in several rules such as— 34, 35, 40, 41, 42.1, 42.2, 42.3, 43, 37.3, 44.1)
Onus of proof	**24**, 121, 128, 136, 137, 170		(Implied or specified in several rules such as—35, 38, 41.3, 42.3, 43.2)
Hailing	**25**, 117, 118, 149, 151, 156, 161, (12.8)	**34**	Hailing (See also—38.4, 40, 42.1, 43, 46, 60, 68.3, 72.4)
Restrictions on altering course Misleading, Balking	**25**, 126, 127, 129, 145, (11.9), 174	**35**	Limitations on altering course
Luffing	**26**, (**2.7**), **117**, (**9.5**), 118, 119, 120, 121, 135, 145, 148, 150, 151, (11.25), 156	**Definition**—Luffing **38**	Same tack—Luffing and sailing above a proper course after starting

Bibliography

Books dealing mainly with racing rules:

Interpretations of the Racing Rules (IYRU, London). Gives details of important protest cases which have gone to Appeal and which have been judged important enough to be generally published.

Paul Elvstrom Explains the Yacht Racing Rules, edited by Richard Creagh-Osborne (Distributed by Creagh-Osborne & Partners, John de Graff Inc. (USA) and Granada Publishing). Complete package in waterproof wallet. Contains facsimile of official rules text, which is revised for every 4-year period, plus commentary and two-colour drawings as well as other information.

The Rules in Action—Eric Twiname (Adlard Coles Ltd.). Analysis of boat-to-boat situations, how the rules work and their tactical implications.

The Rules Book—Eric Twiname (Adlard Coles Ltd.). Small pocket format extracts from 'The Rules in Action'.

Sailing Racing Rules the Easy Way—Stephen Falk (St. Martins Press). A useful and simple explanation of the main right-of-way rules.

The New Yacht Racing Rules—Robert N. Bavier (W.W. Norton & Co.). Sound advice from a very experienced skipper.

The Yacht Racing Rules Today—Bill Bentsen (Dodd, Mead & Company).

Yacht Racing Rules and Tactics—Gordon C. Aymar (Van Nostrand Reinholdt).

Sailboat Racing Rules—Thomas J. McDermott (Quadrangle).

The Rules of Yacht Racing—Bob Smith (Pocket Books Inc.).

Basic Rules of Yacht Racing (with cassette tape) (Sailing Symposiums Inc.).

Books dealing mainly with tactics include:

Tactics and Strategy in Yacht Racing—Joachim Schult (Nautical Publishing & Dodd, Mead & Company).

The Tactics of Small Boat Racing—Dr. Stuart Walker (Hodder & Stoughton & W.W. Norton & Company).

Dinghy Team Racing—Eric Twiname (Adlard Coles Ltd.)

Advanced Racing Tactics—Stuart Walker (W.W. Norton & Company).

Books giving general racing advice:

Start to Win—Eric Twiname (Adlard Coles Ltd.).

Sailing to Win—Robert N. Bavier (W.W. Norton & Company).

Go for the Gold—Garry Hoyt (Nautical Publishing).

Elvstrom Speaks on Yacht Racing (Nautical Publishing).

Winning—John Oakeley (Nautical Publishing).

Sailing from Start to Finish—Yves Louis Pinaud (Adlard Coles Ltd.).

Sail Racer—Jack Knights (Adlard Coles Ltd.).

Small Boat Racing with the Champions—ed. Bob Fisher (Barrie & Jenkins).

179